Queering The Tranny

New Perspectives on Male Transvestism and
Transsexualism

www.queeringthetranny.com

true colours
publishing

First paperback edition printed 2011 in the United Kingdom

Published by True Colours Publishing a division of True Colours Coaching LLP

http://www.truecolourspublishing.com

http://www.queeringthetranny.com

British Library Cataloguing in Publication Data
A catalogue record for this book is available from the British Library

ISBN: 978-0-9565579-9-5

Queering The Tranny

New Perspectives on Male Transvestism and Transsexualism

This above all,

To thine own self be true

And it must follow, as the night the day,

Thou cans't not be false to any man.

(from William Shakespeare's Hamlet)

Glossary

Autogynephillia – Blanchard devised this term when asserting that male transvestites became aroused by the idea of making love to their own female identified or feminised body

Boi – Transgender person presenting a predominantly male identity but generally denoted female at birth

Grrl – Transgender person presenting a predominantly female identity but generally denoted male at birth

Hegemonic – Referring to the way a dominant group exerts control and authority over minority groups and individuals

Heterosexual matrix – This comes from the work of Judith Butler and refers to a seemingly compulsory heterosexuality based on binary gender identities. Later she termed this heterosexual hegemony

Heteronormativity – An underlying assumption that all relationships are by default heterosexual and/or that heterosexuality is the more acceptable identity (and by implication, others are therefore lesser)

Imago – An unconscious image or subconscious fantasy

Kink – Consensual sexual activity that is not merely procreative but recreative. May involve role-play, power play and BDSM

Male-femaling – Richard Ekins' term for male to female gender crossing

Misogyny – The hatred or disavowal of women and femininity

Onanistic – Self pleasuring/masturbatory

Panopticonic – Observed from all directions. More fully explained on p133

'Real Girl' – I use this term slightly sardonically within the text. The context here is that some imagine by dressing as a woman they may become a woman in a very real sense so use the expression "I felt just like a real woman/real girl". Treat all such references as slightly tongue-in-cheek, it's my anarchic humour at play

Sardonic – The use of ironic or dark humour to make a point

Schadenfreude - Taking delight in someone's misfortune

Self-actualisation – This is a humanistic philosophy based on the idea that every human, as an individual, has an inner drive to achieve his or her full potentials and live a full and rich life. That life itself is the endless journey towards that goal

Sin-qua-non – An essential thing

Tranny – A pejorative or derogatory label used to describe any male who presents as female: generally considered offensive today

Zeitgeist – The prevailing or dominant ideas or philosophies of a time or culture

INDEX:

Appendices

PREFACE

For some reading this book there will undoubtedly be curiosity, unfamiliarity, maybe even uneasiness; it might open a door into a world, previously unknown or misunderstood. I guess for some reading it though there will be resonance and maybe similar struggles. In presenting this work then, I have wanted to draw together in a coherent and honest whole, the things that I have learned so that others might have easier access to ideas and experiences than I had when I set out on my journey. I have wanted to bring to a wider audience some of the more abstract and complex ideas that abound in academia, ideas and philosophies which are presented in such complex language they become prohibitive to many readers. And yet language is so important – a word is only ever a symbol of an idea - and if I am to communicate these new and exciting ideas then sometimes it has been necessary to use less common words, even create new words in the service of the communication of a new idea. I hope that you as a reader, will have the patience to bear with me, to refer sometimes to the glossary, even refer to a dictionary where necessary, and ultimately have forgiven me for the times when even I have been guilty of using more abstract vocabulary.

I'd say there is a parallel process here too – one of the biggest problems in terms of understanding transgender is that the word is new and few understand it. When a friend who has known me for years, and who has read my MSc and been introduced to these ideas previously, tells me that 'a creature came in the shop today' she is using the language of a society who does not know how to name and identify gender identities that confuse them. The so-called 'creature' to which she referred was a transsexual woman in her late 60's. And it's not that the friend was being unkind: she just lacked the language. When a bunch of lads on a train see someone who has a beard and a crew cut but is also wearing a skirt and make-up they can only make sense of it by framing this as a 'boy-george'. The language is lacking here, society has new vocabulary to learn. This book attempts to introduce that language, to help introduce the new terms and constructs that will hopefully ultimately break down the barriers to understanding.

Mostly, what I have wanted to achieve in this book is to start to bring some of the more creative, diverse and abstract thoughts and philosophies of gender politics and of post-feminist ideology about sex and sexuality, out into a domain where others outside the realms of academia and living a real existence in a real world might find it; be stimulated by it, and then build on it. I hope it creates in the reader some of the fascination and the curiosity that have been constant drivers for me on the journey that has led to this book and must inevitably continue into the future. I hope you enjoy it. This is not a book of answers per se, it is more a book of ideas, of thoughts and of ways of thinking; ways of conceptualising data and phenomena that can start to transcend the previously 'known' or understood and thereby open up the potential for whole new areas of creativity and new possibilities in the quest for a more honest presentation of self to others in the world. The book in many ways chronicles my own personal quest for a genuine presentation of identity that communicates the inner self – the self that sits between gender binaries; that embraces aspects of humanity and of human identity that have been in a sense culturally denied me by virtue of apparent biological anatomy. In the process of reconstructing my own assumptions about maleness; femaleness; and of challenging my own internal prejudices I have found ways to become more liberated, to live a freer life.

(1997) Ma Vie En Rose

(My Life In Pink)

Ludovic Fabre: I'm a girlboy.

Jérôme: A girlboy?

Ludovic Fabre: To make a baby, parents play tic-tac-toe.
                      When one wins, God sends Xs and Ys.
                      XX for a girl, and XY for a boy. But
                      my X for a girl fell in the trash, and I
                      got a Y instead. See? A scientific
                      error! But God will fix it and send me
                      an X and make me a girl and then we'll
                      get married, okay?

Jerome   That will depend on what kind of girl
                      you are.

                      Director: Alain Berliner,
        Writers: Alain Berliner, Chris Vander Stappen
        Featuring:Georges Du Fresne as Ludovic Fabre
                      Julien Rivière as Jérôme

SECTION 1
Transgender Theory

Why on earth would a man want to dress up like a woman, want to wear 'women's clothes'? It is a question that baffles many; it's a question that had intrigued me for a long time, personally and professionally. A regular theme on problem pages in newspapers and magazines is the wife or girlfriend who comes home to find her partner wearing her clothes: the resultant shock, disgust and confusion almost invariably rocks the relationship to its core. For the men involved there is often shame, secrecy, confusion and fear.

Although, particularly during the second half of the twentieth century, the cultural zeitgeist moved to broaden the scope of the female wardrobe toward an inclusion of traditionally male attire, there has been broadly speaking, no reciprocal move for men. Indeed, when David Beckham puts on a sarong or wears nail varnish he is mocked and ridiculed. And yet, how we make sense of, and present our gendered and sexual selves is a fundamental part of how we are as human beings – key to our relationships with others.

The first section of the book explores the theory of transgender identities, the historical contexts and looks at what current academic and scientific thinking can show us to help us make more sense of this phenomenon. The first half is written in an academic voice and follows the conventions of academic writing: some may find this unfamiliar as a style but I hope to have kept it readable. The second half of the book is in a different style, a different voice. Here auto-ethnography and free flowing informal narrative tells a very personal and more emotional story. As a reader feel free to approach the book in which ever way feels most comfortable or appealing to you. I've tried to keep the chapters of this book relatively short so that it can be read in instalments without the reader losing the overall message. I have taken the opportunity to intersperse chapters and sections with additional quotations to stimulate thought.

I hope you enjoy the journey.

INTRODUCTION

In this first part of the book I present the 'theory'. Well actually I present a chronology of the theory, weighing historical conceptualisations against contemporary ideas and scientific knowledge, to help illustrate that our understanding of the phenomenon of male cross-gender identities is still developing and needs to be understood at multiple levels.

As humans, we can only make sense of our world from the view we have of it at any given time, within our given 'locality'. If in ancient times, primitive people stood on the shore line of an ocean and (knowing only their locality) believed the world to be flat, we can understand how such a straight forward 'common sense' (albeit flawed) deduction arises. How could they possibly comprehend the idea that what appeared to be so obviously flat - was in truth, very not flat: in truth a gentle curve, a curve that when observed from sufficient distance showed its true form as that of a globe. And so to embrace this radical notion of the world as spherical, we had also to revise our understanding of other more fundamental ideas about our world: not least of which was to re-conceptualise the idea that people on the underside of the globe didn't fall off into the sky because gravity pulls us towards the centre and not 'down' into the ground. Even children today struggle to comprehend how this can be true

– and yet as adults we can reference to images of the globe; the Space Program; our experiences of foreign travel; and build an internal model, a way of making sense of it even if it remains rather abstract – what exactly is gravity anyway?

And thus, our straight forward 'common sense' (albeit flawed) ideas about gender, sex, and sexuality might therefore be seen in a similar way - as a local understanding, caught up in the culture, knowledge and experience of the local tribe and therefore subject to the same naive but understandable limitations. We see what is viewable from our particular vantage point: for those who stand on a hill a wider view and other lands are visible, for those of us prepared to travel the oceans, whole new and exotic lands become known and experienced. In writing this, and being aware of the process of writing this, I find an image comes to mind: of the early explorers, people who set sail across great oceans, faced the dangers inherent in the navigation of uncharted seas, in the exploration of new lands, but were prepared to brave those potentially hostile and dangerous environments to discover new things, new peoples, new ideas, new potentials. They would come back from their travels with artefacts from these lands, and in offering these artefacts demonstrate the idea of new potentials, sometimes inspiring others to take the risk, to travel the ocean, to find that land, to find other lands. Sometimes though, taking back that knowledge to the tribe would be harder, more challenging, because it threatened or destabilised their world view and would be met with resistance; hostility. Such is the lot of the adventurer, the explorer, the revolutionary.

And a part of me sometimes feels like that explorer: the theory section of the book perhaps akin to the nautical charts held by the admiralty – this is what we know exits out there and what we think exists. From that place I set sail to chart new lands and found other peoples, other places and in my own way managed to create new territory.

Our knowledge, our 'knowing' of anything is therefore this complex function of how we interpersonally make sense of our individual experience of the world we inhabit, in the context of the accepted knowledge of the local tribe, caught up in the cultural milieu: a function of where we are standing within a locality and yet also enriched by the experiences of the places where we have travelled.   My own understanding of transvestism, transsexualism, transgenderism as individual and co-related phenomena has been repeatedly reconstructed as a result of the travels I have made as part of my research journey, a journey of self exploration, the journey of writing an MSc dissertation, the journey I have taken in writing this book, the journey I continue to make.

Part of the purpose of this book is to describe the amazing finds I made on my journey. To help others know that other lands, other ideas exist, and to make those ideas, those existences and experiences open and available to others who might not otherwise have access to them.

Writing this book has presented a challenge. In the far off lands of academia and political philosophy are extraordinary ideas; notions; ways of explaining and knowing: things that challenge our more primitive explanations. And yet the language and style of so many of these texts and academic research papers is complex, often seemingly prohibitive, excluding. Many of the texts assume prior knowledge or understanding which can make a book title look appealing but the contents remain out of intellectual reach. Oftentimes complex language and terms are used which require continual reference to a large dictionary or in some case a crib-sheet to help. I therefore, in presenting this work to you, have tried to walk a tight-rope - between the world of the academic, where those complex ideas sometimes really do need complex words to properly define them; and the world of the more readable, where people who want to understand, want to learn, can travel and explore and do not feel excluded from the work.

These are early days in the field of transgender: the seas are in many ways uncharted and there are sometimes dangers out there. To discover some of these places requires courage but the rewards are immense.

The Research Journey

My MSc research journey set out to question and explore how counsellors and psychotherapists conceptualise clients who present with sexuality and/or gender diversity issues and to what extent their knowledge is informed by current academic understandings. This first section of this book primarily presents the outcome of the literature review from that project and summary research findings with additional reflections and notes where more recent research has allowed me to expand upon or clarify a point. I have endeavoured to keep the whole book more readable than a typical MSc thesis by limiting the intrusion of data or findings that have greater relevance in other arenas.

As a Cognitive Behavioural Psychotherapist by profession, I was aware that throughout my training there was an absence of any input or reflection on our understanding of Lesbian, Gay, Bisexual and Transgender (LGBT) issues. I recognised and acknowledged that I had never explored the underlying prejudices or ill-informed assumptions related to a same sex attraction or queer identity that I had acquired in my upbringing. Post qualification I started to seek out training in the field of sexual minorities and was able to develop a more specific knowledge related to the particular needs and issues of clients from the Lesbian, Gay, Bisexual, and Transgender (LGBT) community. That in and of itself was a fascinating journey and I am much the richer for having made it. As a result of that post qualification study I also came to recognise that my position on the aetiology of homosexuality for example had to move considerably in the light of contemporary understandings as I increasingly appreciated that much of my previous knowledge was contaminated by the influence of my formative years (the influence of my local tribe). In choosing a specific focus for the dissertation and the research project I chose to consider the presentation of male cross-dressing as a clinical presenting issue. I wanted to challenge and explore the origins of my own disquiet and reactions to this subject and consider these in relation to my changed understanding of homosexuality, and to see how well informed others within the profession were in relation to this subject.

Given that from a Cognitive Behavioural perspective it is argued that our cognitions and internal rules (or schema) shape behavioural and emotional reactions, clearly there are implications for therapeutic work if the counsellor's underlying schema and beliefs are dysfunctional or guided by social (and or internal) prejudice rather than objective understanding. The outcome of this research ultimately demonstrated that many counsellors and psychotherapists are sadly ill informed, and most were able to complete their training without any significant focus on their own internalised homophobia and or address their lack of awareness of sexual minority issues. This has important implications for people from the queer community and especially transgender clients as they seek out therapy to contemplate their self-identity.

In exploring my own understandings, reactions to and perceptions of 'transvestism' I was aware of familial injunctions and messages about 'perverse' [sic] sexualities and homosexuality in particular, and the social conditioning that had been part of my upbringing during the 'homophobic' 1970's and the 'feminism' of the 1980's. My core training as a therapist (1997-2001) had never explicitly addressed these topics although I was influenced by three significant texts recommended to course participants: 'Families and How to Survive them' Skinner & Cleese (1983), 'They Fuck You Up' James (2002) and the Mental Health manual DSM-IV (APA 1994). These texts took a pathological approach to non-hegemonic sexuality, so if anything compounded my prejudice, tempering it with 'scientific' justification.

However, the latest research significantly challenges this view. Indeed, a recent BACP paper looking at counselling provision for clients with LGBT issues emphasises the point:

> *"psychotherapeutic practice that pathologises homosexuality, bisexuality and transgenderism should be replaced by more modern understandings of sexual identity" King et al (2007: p3)*

In acknowledging my own prejudice I felt sure I could put it aside to maintain humanistic values when counselling, however, Denman (2004) argues:

> *"Neither neutrality nor ignorance are helpful adjuncts to the treatment of these conditions. Successful therapy with TG, TV and inter-sex patients needs to be conducted from a position*

*that is well informed about the condition and benignly disposed
towards the client" p249*

remarking that therapists are subject to the same cultural
influences and prejudices as the rest of society and that this
should be tackled in training (a point re-iterated in Haslam 2001;
King 2003; Suthrell 2004; Martell et al 2004; King et al. 2007).

Even if our core training did address sexual minority issues,
understandings have moved on recently. Bond (2004) makes the
case for therapists to use continuing professional development as
a space to engage in, and keep abreast of new developments in
research:

> *"the public standing of counselling and psychotherapy requires
> that practitioners systematically and continually seek to
> enhance the quality, effectiveness and safety of their practice on
> well-founded research" (2004: p2)*

In discussing the outline of this project initially with colleagues, I
discovered that male cross-dressing as a clinical presenting issue
is not that uncommon. Actual figures on the incidence of male
cross-dressing vary considerably though. Acroyd (1979) suggests
1-3%, Gosselin & Wilson (1980)   2-5%; Coleman (1980) 10%;
Bloom (2002) 3%, Reed (2006) 0.7-2%; Ekins (1997) simply states it
is 'widespread'. Bullough & Bullough (1993) point out that given
the secretive nature of transvestite behaviour and the social
unacceptability of being 'out' it is hard to ascertain a true figure
adding that much of the clinically reported material has been
based on clients who presented with psychological dysfunction

to psychiatrists who were already working from their own conceptualisations.

What is clear is that the crossing of gendered identities through the adoption of the clothes of the other, is an historically and cross-culturally constant phenomenon. (see Acroyd 1979; Bullough & Bullough 1993; Herdt 1996; Ramet 1996; Bullough et al 1997; Garber 1997; Fausto-Sterling 2000; Peakman 2004; Suthrell 2004). Whilst many other cultures have integrated 'third sex' categories (see appendix 3), within Western culture, it is almost taboo. Where it has involved women presenting and living as men this has tended to be slightly less problematic (and seen as 'trading up': see Bullough & Bullough 1993; Herdt1996; Garber 1997; Suthrell 2004) whereas for men it has invariably been seen as pathological and more often than not interpreted as related to homosexuality. (Which has never been illegal for lesbians, only men).

As Dzelme & Jones (2001) state:

> *"Cross-dressing is an issue shrouded in confusion and misunderstanding which often leads to cross-dressers seeking therapy."* P293

In this text I shall use the terms transvestite, cross-dresser and transgender person broadly in line with the way the cited author has used them. There is still some debate about nomenclature although increasingly transvestite is seen in a pejorative way by the community, and as theorists increasingly come to the notion that transvestism/cross dressing and transsexualism are part of a continuum the term 'transgender person' becomes a catch-all with neutral association.

Literature Review:

Preface

Having acknowledged to myself that my understanding of male cross-dressing was distorted with negative cultural messages and internalised unease, I set out to learn more about the phenomenon. Of the numerous books available to the counsellor and therapist to guide therapeutic protocols and develop understanding of aetiologies and underlying mechanisms for most presenting issues, there are virtually none relating to male cross-dressing. It became clear that my literature search strategies would need to be diverse and broad ranging - that a balanced, objective position would need to take in many inter-related fields and areas of study. The more I read, the more I discovered new areas of investigation; new philosophies; new ways of looking, not only at this phenomenon, but of how to view research itself and the process of research.

Methodology

Combinations therefore, of academic database searches, web search, and citation tracking methods were used to accumulate the body of research material that informed the MSc study initially, and then was later extended to build the theory section of this book. The process of building the research data and pursuing Internet searches (through such tools as Google Scholar) was conducted over an extended period of approximately five years leading up to the publication of this work. Citation tracking proved particularly effective in linking to other relevant research and texts.

Findings

Male cross-dressing, despite being a common theme in problem pages has only infrequently been the focus of serious academic research. Quite why this is the case is hard to say, although as Suthrell (2004) notes

> *"friends expressed their surprise that I should want to study such a bizarre group, with their undertones of underground-verging-on-deviant lifestyles" p3*

Reisbig (2007) remarks that a lack of literature makes it harder for therapists to be appropriately informed and that this has a negative impact on therapeutic interventions. That said, there is a wealth of literature on sexuality and gender studies and it is predominantly from these areas that I have been able to draw both explicitly and implicitly in understanding the phenomenon of why some men are so driven to wear the clothes of the opposite biological sex, despite the potential negative consequences.

In an analysis of over a hundred texts and academic papers on the subjects of sex, sexuality and gender the following themes emerged. Understandings on the aetiology of transvestism and transsexualism, fell broadly into three camps - the biological (neuro-hormonal; genetic), the Social Constructionist/Feminist and the Psychodynamic/Psychoanalytic. The latter, initiated chiefly by Ellis (1959) Storr (1964) and Stoller (1968) seemed to have influenced 'the medical model' and contemporary texts on sexual deviancy or sexual deviation have still referred back to these authors, emphasising the pathological and fetishistic aspects- suggesting transvestism is an un-natural part-object sexuality caused chiefly by parental dynamic (Laws & O'Donohue 1997; Rosen 1996; McConaghy 1993 among others). These authors have often recommended extreme and bizarre treatment protocols involving the use of such things as humiliation of the client, use of emetics, electric shocks applied to the genitals (McConaghy 1993, Zucker & Blanchard 1996,); Electro-Convulsive Therapy (Brierly 1979) and even castration (Stoller 1968)! Ultimately, McConaghy concedes defeat stating that psychotherapy was ineffective in eliminating cross-dressing behaviour leaving him to conclude:

> *"behaviour therapies are markedly less effective in giving transvestites control over the behaviour as compared to exhibitionists and voyeurs, suggesting that biological as compared to learned factors play a stronger role in transvestism"* (1993: p173)

Interestingly, DSM-IV (Morrison 1995, APA 1994) presents 'transvestic fetishism' as a diagnosis of mental illness only in heterosexual men who wear clothes of the opposite sex , since being female or gay excludes one from the criteria. (For a critique of the diagnostic criteria and their application to a case scenario see Moser & Kleinplatz 2002). Recognising that the researchers cited so far were coming from a culturally hetero-normative framework we might consider how this influenced their work. Indeed, it is interesting to note that the dissenting voices historically were researchers such as Hirschfield, and Kinsey and who were acknowledged to have somewhat atypical sexualities.

The notion of transvestism as mental illness and/or sickness is exemplified in Arndt (1991: p77) who says

> *"Psychiatrists consider transvestites more as ill or disabled than as sexual criminals"*

Morrison (1995) describing transvestic fetishism, infers the category covers all men who cross dress going on to suggest *"some patients have been previously involved in rape, exhibitionism or paedophilia."* This paints neither an encouraging nor accurate picture. Bolin (1994) proscribing the notion of transgenderism as illness says:

> *"Ten years ago transsexualism supported the binary gender schema by dividing gender dysphoric individuals into transvestites who were 'sick' or transsexuals who were unfortunates, women trapped in men's bodies" p482*

and argues that 'transgenderists' need to 'come-out' in the way homosexuality had to come-out to gain acceptance and generate understanding. Research by Howells (1984) and Brown et al (1996) challenges the notion that transvestite men are psychopathologically any different to the more general male population, (and are therefore not 'ill') a point re-iterated in Moser & Kleinplatz (2002) who argue that diagnostic criteria create the problem, not the cross-dressing. Lance (2002) in a project set within an American educational campus, illustrated that intolerance towards homosexual students (and their resultant psychological distress) was reduced through the delivery of a program of education about, and awareness of LGBT issues to the wider college population. This he proposes as a model for society more generally with regard to transgenderism.

Historical Conceptualisations:

Ekins (1997) makes the point that the 'medical model' dominant until recently was conceptualised from within the historical, biological and psychological understandings of the time. Since sexual minorities had not been explored or understood from within, they could not develop their own legitimacy. It's a classic Catch-22. Ramet (1996) notes that it is chiefly Western and Christian culture that has attached gender to the notion of 'biological' sex dimorphism noting as others do that the Christian faith, unlike other faith systems, avoids presenting intersex or cross-gendered icons and 'forbids' cross-dressing through a section in the Bible under Deuteronomy 22:5. (see Whittle 2000; Fausto-Sterling 2000). If the dominant discourses of Western culture through the earlier part of the twentieth century were caught up in patriarchy and the religious doctrine of Christianity, (and thus tending perhaps towards a notion of 'sex' as procreation not recreation and hetero-sexuality as part of the 'natural order of things') it starts to make sense that gender images and sexualities that deviated from that 'natural' logic would be deemed un-natural or pathological. Similarly, if we give consideration to Butler's (2007) description of 'gender' as the 'sexualisation of the inequality of men and women' (pxiii) we might understand the way in which it becomes the enforced and enforcing paradigm, given the almost exclusively male ownership of Religious, Governmental, Medical and Psychiatric institutions. Might this also explain the greater fear within men of homosexuality and effeminacy, associated as they are with subordination and weakness (Suthrell 2004; Bader 2003; O'Keefe 1999)?

Working from within these cultural zeitgeists and viewing the phenomenon of transgenderism and homosexuality through a hetero-normative lens, it is understandable that early theorists looked to find 'causes' for these atypical sexualities rather than simply acknowledge, name and understand them.

Although Kinsey et al (1953) had not specifically investigated transvestites as a group per se he did challenge the perception that transvestites were 'repressed homosexuals', describing these as entirely separate phenomenon. Interestingly, so pervasive was the 'repressed homosexual' argument that as Bullough & Bullough (1993) comment, *"even if the client claimed he was heterosexual the psychoanalyst could still label him as a latent homosexual."*. *p216*

Magnus Hirschfield in 1938 (see Bullough & Bullough 1993; Whittel 2000) had differentiated transvestism as separate from homosexuality repressed or otherwise and it was he who coined the phrase 'transvestism' (literally cross-clothing). Havellock Ellis, one of the leading sex researchers of his time, described transvestism as a form of what he termed Sexo-aesthetic inversion (Ellis 1953). Seeing it as more complex than simply adopting the clothes of the opposite sex (transvestism), he coined the phrase 'Eonism' after the Chevalier d'Eon an eighteenth century diplomat who despite being biologically male had lived much of his life presenting to the world as female through attire and mannerism. Ellis noted that generally transvestites were heterosexual in orientation but suggested a strong identification with the mother possibly due to an over-close attachment. He also noted that, like homosexuality, it was not apparently curable. Storr (1964) takes a much more pejorative and dogmatic slant on things suggesting that castration anxiety and a failed Oedipal resolution explain the phenomenon. His assertion is that the transvestite is trying to create an idealised fantasy woman because of innate 'inhibitions and fears in any sexual situation with a real woman'. He states that it is the mother who 'wears the trousers' in the home of the transvestite and that at some level he is identifying with this powerful dominant (and therefore 'phallic') woman rather than the 'inadequate' father. (Note that this follows Lacanian thought - the phallus is associated with, or more correctly symbolises, ownership of power and dominance, rather than the notion merely of possessing a penis per se: which, set within a patriarchal milieu, becomes a logical albeit flawed corollary.) With extraordinary conviction he asserts that transvestites have thus overcome their castration anxiety through identification with this 'phallic woman'. He ultimately describes it as 'emotional immaturity of a rather profound kind' (1964: p62).

Stoller (1964) interestingly took a multi-factorial approach to the phenomenon, arguing that:

> *" The sense of maleness is present and permanent from earliest life and that the penis is not essential to this sense of maleness"*
> *p4*

He cited the case of two boys who, due to birth abnormalities were born without penises and yet clearly identified as male and engaged in masculine behaviours. Stoller did align though to the passive father and dominant mother argument, popular then, asserting that the mothers of transvestites had secretly wanted girls and had dressed these boys in female attire when the fathers were not around. Interestingly, Prince (in Arndt 1991) was later able to dispute this assertion finding only 4% of his survey of cross-dressers reported this experience.

Roiphe and Galenson (1981) again emphasise the significance of parental dynamics although without demonstrating meaningful clinical data asserting that:

> "*the importance of paternal availability and support for the boy's growing sense of his male sexual identity during the second part of the second year of life cannot be too strongly stressed*" p273

What they don't do is explain for example, how the sons of service personnel manage to develop healthily when many will have experienced fathers away from home for extended periods. Similarly, given the incidence of single parent families, particularly 'single mother-absent father' families that have become increasingly common in the last thirty years, might we expect to be 'over-run' with effeminate men by now?

Bullough et al (1983) challenging these explanations make reference to earlier work re-iterating the dominant-mother-absent-father conceptualisation:

"The so-called 'Bieber Mom' the dominant, overprotective, and close binding woman who superintended a family situation sufficiently pathological to induce sexual variation in her child, has been utilized to explain transvestism and transsexualism (Bieber, 1962, 1968)" p241

concluding from their own data that absent fathers were no more common among the sexual minority groups than they were in the general population.

Limentani (1998) coins the phrase 'vagina man' as his reciprocation to the phallic woman - a man who appears masculine but suffers from a psychic femininity due to an overpowering and symbiotic mother, thus becoming the:

".. mother's treasured phallus, his fate sealed by age 2 or 3 by excluded father and lack of oedipal relationship." p135

Mitchell (2000) agrees with Limentani suggesting the 'vagina man':

"escapes overwhelming primitive anxiety by identifying with an undifferentiated protector...an identification with the otherwise lost object he needs - the woman as mother" p261

Other contemporary authors have perpetuated this conceptualisation. As cited earlier, Skinner & Cleese (1983) and James (2002) dismissed biological factors in favour of the unresolved Oedipal issues scenario.

Maguire (2004) asserts that the effeminate boy is reacting to 'familial trauma':

> *"His 'girlish' persona may represent a desperate attempt to keep an abandoning or rejecting mother inside his psyche"p44*

However, the clinical evidence base for these assertions is lean to say the least and at some level they have perhaps only sustained themselves through a process of self-reinforcement. Martell et al (2004) make the point that until recently certain schools of therapy (particularly psychoanalytic) would not admit openly homosexual therapists on to the training courses since anything less than heterosexual orientation was deemed 'immature' and thus the individual was considered 'impaired'. You'd need to be 'cured' or 'normal' before you could join and thus a circular argument is created. Increasingly researchers have used more scientific methods to challenge psychoanalytic conceptualisations. Acroyd (1979) describes evidence to back psychoanalytic explanations as 'not convincing', an outcome later repeated and echoed by Bullough et al (1983) and Schott (1995), the former concluding that:

> *"the psychoanalytic picture of the domineering mother and weak or absent father was not supported by the data",p249*

If, even as early as 1949, Cauldwell had argued that trying to treat transvestism was *'as foolish as trying to treat some star to behave differently in the solar system'*. What sense might we make of its aetiology and manifestations and how might we regard it?

Contemporary understandings:

Increasingly, theorists are suggesting the possible influence of pre-natal hormonal environments and genetic predispositions as formative in the phenomenon of gendered behaviours and thus transgenderism. Interestingly, ultimately aligned to the biological influence theorists was Money (1995) who gained considerable attention earlier in his career through what has now come to be known as the 'notorious' John/Joan case. (as detailed in Appendix 2). Originally supporting a notion that gender identity was entirely socially defined, he has since implicated the influence of prenatal hormones and maternal stress during key points in the pregnancy on gendered behaviour of the infant suggesting a 'critical phase' hypothesis. This view is supported by McConaghy (1993) who notes that even Freud originally suggested 'constitutional and experiential elements' in the development of homosexuality and transsexualism, and cites research from as early as 1953 (Bakwin and Bakwin 1953) which proposed a biological mechanism behind homosexual and trans-gendered identity/behaviour, challenging the underlying model of the time which was more focussed on the family dynamics.

Brizendine (2007) argues that at the heart of enduring misunderstandings about female [and implicitly male] psychology was the mistaken belief that women were merely 'small men'. Moir & Moir (1998) similarly note how political correctness confused equality with sameness and argue that biologically male and female brains are structurally and functionally different, a theme extended by Pinker (2008) and Brizendine (2007) who makes the point:

"Until eight weeks old every brain looks female - female is nature's default gender setting.   A huge testosterone surge beginning in the eighth week will turn this unisex brain male". p14

Citing the example of girls born with the intersex condition 'congenital adrenal hyperplasia' (masculinisation of the female genitalia in an X-X foetus) she asserts that prenatal hormonal environments affect the outcome on key identifiers such as 'rough and tumble play' (see also Jurgensen et al 2007). Evidence for the influence of prenatal hormones at critical developmental phases is also put forward by Howells (1984); Durden-Smith & deSimone (1983); Mustanski et al (2002); Baron-Cohen (2004); Lippa (2005); Rammsayer & Troche (2006); Manning (2008) and Auyung et al (2009). As an additional point of interest here, some of this research arises through the study of human intersex conditions and for further information on this phenomenon you may wish to refer to O'Keefe (1999); Lippa (2005); Fausto-Sterling (2000).

Kruijver et al (2000) investigated a specific portion of the brain (the bed nucleus of the stria terminalis) and identified significant differences between male brains, and those of male-to-female transsexuals noting the latter closely matched more typically female patterns. Wilson et al (2002) investigating the same area of the brain present findings suggesting these brain sex differences develop over a period possibly extending into adulthood but is defined and influenced by prenatal elements.

Lippa (2005) suggests the middle third of pregnancy as potentially critical to brain-based gender identity. Suggesting

DNA as a human 'recipe' (and using a cake baking analogy) he argues that external conditions such as hormones and early rearing can significantly affect the outcome. Gosselin & Wilson (1980), supporting the argument for a combination of genetic and environmental components, comment on the greater vulnerability of the male foetus to environmental variables in-utero (given that all foetuses start as female and need to become masculinised through a series of hormonal developmental phases). It is already widely acknowledged that male children are more likely to suffer from autism, dyslexia, ADHD and left-handedness, and theories on the aetiology on these include brain development trauma and 'developmental instability' during pregnancy. It is interesting to note that there is a significantly higher incidence of left-handedness in homosexual and transsexual males than the general population (see Coren 1982; Howells 1984; McManus 2002; Reed 2006; Blanchard & Lippa 2007; Manning 2008).

Mustanski et al (2002) find strong evidence to support the influence of genetics and some evidence to support hormonal influences in the development of sexual and gendered behaviour, particularly in male foetuses. Howells (1984) suggests minor damage to the left side of the brain, as *"more likely to result in bizarre or unorthodox targets for sexual arousal"* which if true, is interesting given that left-handed males are right brain dominant. Coren (1982) cites research linking testosterone levels in-utero to developmental problems with the left hemisphere implicating this in the aetiology of left-handedness. Recent work by Professor Simon Baron-Cohen (2004) and his team (see also Auyung et al 2009; Auyung et al 2010) has presented evidence indicating a strong link between autism and a hyper-masculinized brain pattern arising from high levels of prenatal androgen.

Although searching for biological aetiologies is controversial (given that it can be used as an argument to find 'cures' or to eliminate certain sub-groups from society) I assert that it can also be of value if it challenges those who believe the symptoms are merely 'narcissistic choice'. I would ultimately concur with Bullough & Bullough (1993), who argue that whilst evidence for genetic and physiological precursors has been 'growing over the last two decades' their conclusion is that:

> *"Gender identity is apparently the product of a complex interaction among three factors - a genetic predisposition, physiological factors and the socialization process" p313.*

If, as seems to be the case, sexual orientation and gendered behaviours are separately defined aspects of brain development, what implications does this have for the male child who has a brain more oriented towards the feminine developmental pattern?

Social Constructionism - The 'Self' defined through family, school and society:

As my research journey has increasingly illustrated to me the complexity and diversity of the origins of the gendered and sexual self, I am reminded of a remark by a lesbian friend of mine some years ago.

"God's idea of a joke was to create ten different sexes and then call them 'man' and 'woman'"

Dzelme & Jones (2001) comment:

"At birth, society and family begin the pattern of mapping out the appropriate gender role" p294

I have always been aware of the very narrow bandwidth of socially acceptable masculine identity. In school in the 1970's, there were clear delineations between male and female, enforced mostly by the social group with threats of being identified as 'poof''; 'sissy'; 'queer'; or 'gay' for any non-conformity. It seems little has changed in the past thirty years (see Frosh et al 2002; Renold 2005; Lippa 2005). Recent research in schools looking at the development of gendered and sexual identities by these authors shows that 'homophobia' is still rife (and at some level still officially sanctioned) although it is fairer to say that it refers more to non-masculine behaviour rather than a perception that the boy accused is sexually attracted to other boys. As Renold (2005) identifies it was

"children who actively persisted to subvert and resist dominant and hegemonic identities who were routinely targeted [for bullying]; P82

It remains the case then that the main way of defining masculinity and boy-ness is in opposition to feminine, leading to an essential suppression of the feminine for fear of exposure, ridicule and rejection. In endeavouring to understand the need for a male to adopt the clothing and or part time identity of a woman we might consider the internal conflict and shame between these internalised messages about acceptable identities and the inner experiencing of the self. For the girl who wishes to explore and at some level express her masculine elements is the option of the tom-boy which seems to have greater social acceptability. (see Hite 1981; Woodhouse 1989; Ramet 1996; Atkinson et al 1996; Garber 1997; Wilson & Rahman 2005; Moorhead 2007). For boys wishing to identify with or venture into any part of 'girl-world' comes the rejection of the peer group and the threat of physical violence. Haywood & Mac an Ghaill (2003) describe the use of physical violence to reinforce 'appropriate maleness' within boyhood school culture; the notion of femininity (and therefore by implication homosexuality) becoming 'structuring anxieties' for men (see also Denman 2004; Schaivi 2004). Boys who wish to express aspects of a feminine self may also experience rejection from fathers (Atkinson et al 1996) indeed, an interesting counter to the dominant-mother-absent-father model is put forward by Wilson & Rahman (2005) who suggest that it is fathers who withdraw from their effeminate sons. Roiphe & Galenson (1981) comment on the overt and covert gendered socialisation process of children by their parents: a point re-iterated in Chesser (1964) who remarks that the:

> " *child learns to adapt behaviour to accord with parental non-verbal cues*" *p147*

Schaivi (2004) coins the phrase effeminaphobia to describe the social (and here I would add paternal) discomfort with 'effeminate' boys saying:

"If a girl-boy has any story to tell it would seem to be that of compulsory integration within recognizable narrative passages of heterosexual love and family" (2004: p1)

Ramet (1996) describes 'gender' as being 'the very core of an individual's self-definition' and identity. Devor (2004) suggests that within the self is a 'deep need to be witnessed by others for whom we are' but notes that intense social disapproval of effeminate behaviour in men constrains this. Suthrell (2004) remarks,

" For males to espouse female traits is somehow not only pointless but deeply ridiculous – in an unacceptable way..." p154

Others comment on the social injunctions against males adopting cross-gendered identities, using such terms as "silly; freakish; funny; deviant; perverted; un-natural; un-manly; repulsive; morally perverse; wierdos; queers" (Acroyd 1979; Woodhouse 1989; Peakman 2004; Bloom 2002; Perlman 2003; Ekins 1997). So that perhaps as Bullough & Bullough (1993) remark:

"This perceived unwillingness of society to allow males to express what society has labelled a feminine side is more a pathology of our society than of the individual" p363

Given the social stigma associated with the expression of femininity in boys it seems hardly surprising that the male who experiences the world through a brain that bio-psychically sits somewhere between the binary divide (male-or-female) is faced with an impossible dilemma, which Lee (2005) describes as the 'beach-ball held under water' scenario: it takes a lot of energy to keep it hidden and eventually it needs to surface in some way. Butler (1993, 2007) describes 'gender' as 'performed; reiterative'; arguing that:

> "*Heterosexual gender norms produce inapproximable ideals, heterosexuality can be said to operate through the regulated production of 'man ' and 'woman'. These are for the most part compulsory performances, ones which none of us choose but which each of us is forced to negotiate." (1993: p237).*

I concur, although suggest that women have greater freedom through the advancement of feminism to perform a more diverse 'femininity' than men do their 'masculinity'.

Cross-dressing carries with it great internalised shame (Bullough and Bullough 1993; Martell et al 1994; Schott 1995; Suthrell 2004; Lippa 2005), perhaps because historically it has been associated with homosexuality and or fetishistic and thereby masturbatory fantasies. Generally conducted in secret, as Reisbig (2007) points out, the clinical samples historically may not be truly representative of the more general transgendered and cross-dressing population.

For the male with a strong desire to experience a feminine aspect of self against these cultural injunctions, the social disapproval, and messages of internal shame, it seems reasonable to deduce that occasions to cross-dress become highly charged events emotionally and therefore sexually. It is understandable but incorrect to assume that the cross-dressing is invariably fetishistic. As Lee (2005) points out, there is no reason to believe that there are any more fetishists in the cross-dressing community than in the male population as a whole. Ekins (1997) from his extensive study and involvement in the transgendered community, reports that when opportunities for dressing are more frequent and less covert, the sexual element becomes un-important, and these men simply describe a sense of 'inner peace' when dressed - an escape from the demands of 'performing' the false 'masculine' self. Bullough et al (1983) comparing transsexuals with transvestites, found that:

> "*Transvestites were eminently successful, were heavily into male identified occupations, and, outwardly, seemed secure in their role as males. Perhaps the very security of success in the male world carries a burden which the adoption of a feminine persona allows them to escape*". *p250*

Moser & Kleinplatz (2002) suggest therapists challenge their preconceptions about the maladaptivity of cross-dressing, arguing that there is no empirical evidence that it is problematic or a mental disorder. Whilst I agree with the latter I assert that it is naive to assume that it is not problematic for many. The cross-dresser has to work within the limitations and prejudice of current society - walking down the street cross-dressed is not always necessarily safe (Eddie Izzard describes being beaten up for being cross dressed (Izzard et al 1998); Vicky Lee (2005) suggests using a taxi to move between T-girl friendly hotel and trans-venue). And few are fortunate enough to have a partner who can manage to do any more than perhaps tolerate the behaviour.

Conclusions arising from the review of available literature:

What has ultimately become clear to me as a researcher, is that 'transvestism' per se, is not a single or fixed entity but one with complex manifestations: further, its aetiology remains to some extent disputed. A comprehensive review of the literature has failed to find substantiated evidence to support earlier notions of dysfunctional parental dynamics (dominant mother-weak father hypothesis; mother dressing boy as girl scenario). There is however sufficient evidence from other research to clearly dispute these early theories. Feminism and Social Constructionism as philosophical schools have suggested that all gendered behaviours were learned and conditioned through the socialisation process and we still have authors such as Fine (2010) clinging on to these arguments. I have previously been strongly influenced by these ideologies: however, this has run contrary to the experience of even feminist friends of mine who, as parents, have sometimes despaired at an apparent default programming in their children's behaviours and attitudes. Current research investigating brain development and function is increasingly demonstrating structural differences between typically male and female brains, and that behavioural traits previously assumed to be socially conditioned, are to some extent at least, almost certainly hard wired. (see Holt &Ellis 1998; Whittle 2000; Baron-Cohen (2004); Blanchard & Lippa 2007; Manning 2008; Pinker (2008); Auyeung et al 2009).

These are hotly debated arguments though and I understand the feminist concern that scientific knowledge might be used to justify disadvantage, discrimination and even oppression. Scientific 'facts' have throughout history been used to justify mistreatment of minority groups and I include a brief selection of quotes relating to gender non-conformity and homosexuality to illustrate this in appendix 1. I acknowledge the concern, but assert that scientific truism does not have to imply hierarchical disadvantage: I'd say both sexes lose if we assert that 'equal' has to mean 'same'. Ultimately, a key tenet of this book is that 'masculine' and 'feminine' as gender identified traits can exist beyond the genital anatomy – that femaleness can exist in a male body; that maleness can exist in a female body, and that in an ideal world a degree of gender fluidity would be more easily tolerated and accepted. In the deconstruction then of gender would lay true equality.

Although for a long time, gender non-conforming males have been defined according the constructs of transvestite or transsexual, and therefore seen as separate phenomenon, I believe there is good reason to support the argument of contemporary authors who suggest conceptualising transvestism and transsexualism on a 'transgender continuum'. [See for example authors like Bolin (1998), Bornstein (1998), Denman (2004), Lee (2005); and so called 'queer theorists' mentioned later]. To set this in context: historically there was a necessary divide between the two, chiefly due to the diagnostic criteria the medical profession set for transsexualism. To 'qualify' as a transsexual and thereby access Sex-Reassignment programs one needed to clearly distinguish oneself from the 'transvestite' group. Known as 'learning the script' (O'Keefe 1999) one had to present a coherent and acceptable narrative or risk losing access to hormonal treatment and ultimately surgery (see also Zandvliet 2000). Further, since medical (and thereby social) understanding of the phenomenon had been shaped strongly by the historical pathologising approach we might consider carefully the personal and professional epistemologies underpinning our work. Heron & Reason (1997) describe the way 'propositional knowledge' (underlying theory/intellectual conceptualisation) shapes the way we describe our 'experiencing' both to ourselves and to others, and thereby distort it through a process of filtered interpretation and reiteration.

Therefore, whether personally or indeed professionally, we need to consider our frame of reference carefully, before accepting and re-imposing/self-imposing these historic labels (that someone is simply transvestite or transsexual) and think more about the context of how this supposed understanding or knowledge was developed and informed. This argument will particularly apply if we are approaching this from a psychotherapeutic perspective: when hearing and interpreting our client narratives, we need as therapists to be taking account of how our clients (transvestite; transsexual; transgendered) will inevitably be influenced by this same cultural milieu, incorporating at some level, the social constructions that are part of that, and an emerging LGBT scene. For example, Grayson Perry describes how he 'discovered' that what he was doing was called 'transvestism' by reading an article in the 'News Of The World' when he was 15 (Jones & Perry 2006: p73). I would suggest that the Foucaultian argument applies here: if a label identity such as 'homosexuality', is socially constructed to define an outlawed practice (see Spargo 1999), might we not also see a parallel apply equally here: that the use of the labels 'transvestite'/ 'transsexual' are ultimately unhelpful to us for similar reasons. This is particularly so for therapists if they are to remain open to truly understanding the client and avoid reinforcing and reiterating social stigma and constraining paradigm. What emerges from the literature is that transgenderism provides a more effective construct for conceptualising a spectrum of people who don't neatly fit the hetero-normative binary. An exciting new philosophy is emerging in the form of so called 'Queer theory' with authors like Bolin (1997), Bornstein (1994, 1998), O'Keefe & Fox (2003), Wilchins (2004) arguing in favour of creating new paradigms around gender-pluralism to allow people to express their gender in more diverse ways: I would like to think that within the counselling and psychotherapy profession, and ultimately within society more generally, we might embrace some of these ideologies, recognising but challenging the cultural limits that impact on us all, and working towards a way of helping gender divergent clients become more self actualised. (see also Fee 2006, Zandvliet 2000)

Summary:
Based on a thorough and extensive analysis of the literature available I summarise my findings thus:
- Evidence suggests that male transgenderism is a complex and fixed phenomenon as intrinsic as (but separate from) sexual orientation.
- A neuro-hormonal and/or genetic aetiological paradigm compounded by the social milieu provides the most credible explanation of the phenomenon to date.
- Clinical studies have shown that male cross-dressing should not be seen as a symptom of psychological dysfunction in itself. However, complications arising from intolerance towards male gender diversity may lead some clients to suffer psychological distress - for example

though marital discord; discrimination in the workplace; bullying and harassment.

- Previous conceptualisations regarding the aetiology of transvestism as being a function of parent-child dynamics are no longer useful or valid to us as practitioners.
- Societal expectations of males to 'perform masculine' (and disassociate from feminine and or effeminate) creates internal tension for some men. This may be stronger in a male with a brain that has retained some elements of the primary female developmental patterns.
- The psychiatric paradigm of male transvestism as 'paraphilia' (thus fetishistic) does not fit the data from research in non-clinical transgender male client groups and is likely to relate only to a small sub-group of this population.
- Transgendered males might be defining themselves according to the dominant discourses of 'transvestite' or 'trans-sexual' and may narrate their stories according to these 'scripts'. They may not be aware of contemporary and developing discourses of gender-pluralism and indeed transgenderism itself, which offer healthier less pathological ways of interpreting their experience.
- In the absence of any appreciable awareness – by either client or therapist, of gender-queer and transgender as legitimate and healthy identities, there will inevitably be significant implications for the counselling profession in terms of how we might explore and make sense of our clients and their stories, and thus, how we reflect that back in the process of therapy.

MSc Research findings (see Drummond 2008):

Ultimately, what emerges from the study is that few courses seem to address issues of sexuality and/or gender diversity explicitly. Where it is addressed, it appears from discussions arising from this study to often be as a result of an LGBT sympathetic tutor including it in an ad-hoc way, and less so, as a result of a formal curriculum. The Shaw et al (2008) study supports this finding and makes the point - as others do (Barker 2007, Fee 2006, Walker 2000, Davies & Neal 2000b). - that therapists are subject to the same prejudices and biases as others and that colleges should be addressing this unacknowledged hetero-sexism.

As Maguire (2004) writes:

> *"hopefully, as psychotherapists continue to abandon some of our more facile assumptions about what constitutes 'normal' sexuality, we will be able to acknowledge that such changes may well offer new possibilities for sexual happiness, a more open way of being for all of us" p209*

Spargo (1999) writes

> *"The thoughts I have are bound up with my society's constructions of reality... so I perceive my sexual identity within the set of options determined by a cultural network of discourses" p52*

Some of the therapist comments in the survey were very much caught up in this idea of 'socially constructed reality', their frame of reference turned to the visual aesthetic of the transgender male, wanting them to 'look convincing' (as 'women'); have 'shaved legs'. These cultural rules, 'propositions' (to use Heron & Reason's 1997 model) shape for all of us the practice of our gendered self. Butler's (1993) notion of a 'hetero-sexual matrix': a culturally defined set of behaviours; attributes; shaped experiencing: defining and defined as Male-or-Female constrains us to these ways of understanding our world and sets injunctions against transgressors. Stone (1998) invites the reader to compare our treatment of transgendered identities today with another biological anomaly left-handedness:

> *"Their innate gender behaviour is something like being born left-handed. Think of all the "sinister" stereotypes that have traditionally been associated with left-handedness, and the unnecessary discipline and punishments we visited on left-handed children."*

When as a child I moved to a school in Scotland, the first encounter I had in the playground was with a large gang demanding to know: "So are you Catholic or Protestant?" Asked with some menace, I remember being frightened and somewhat confused. Having been raised atheist I had no idea so I replied, "I don't know, what's the difference?" The shock to them was palpable, how could this kid not know? It confused them sufficiently to spare me the beating they had intended: I sat in a place religiously that was outside their experience, outside their frames of reference. But I existed nonetheless.

When I started this journey, like many, I knew of only transvestite or transsexual as identities for gender non-conforming males, transgender sat outside my frames of reference. What I learned is that Transgender exists nonetheless, and that transgender as a concept and a way of being offers the potential for a more congruent self.

SECTION TWO

Doing Transgender

Carl Rogers, humanist and philosopher wrote:

"I believe it will be clear that a person who is involved in the directional process which I have termed the good life is a creative person. With his sensitive openness to his world, his trust of his own ability to form new relationships with his environment, he would be the type of person from whom creative products and creative living emerge. He would not necessarily be 'adjusted ' to his culture, and he would almost certainly not be a conformist. But at any time and in any culture he would live constructively, in as much harmony with his culture as a balanced satisfaction of needs demanded. In some cultural situations he might in some ways be very unhappy, but he would continue to move toward becoming himself, and to behave in such a way as to provide the maximum satisfaction of his deepest needs. Such a person would I believe, be recognised by the student of evolution as the type most likely to adapt and survive under changing environmental conditions. He would be able creatively to make sound adjustments to new as well as old conditions. He would be a fit vanguard of human evolution."

(from Kirschenbaum & Henderson 1990: P418)

First time out

I remember the first day I actually wore a skirt out – as in properly OUT. Out on the streets; in public as 'Trans'.

I'd been building up to this day for a long time. The journey from 'closet' to a more integrated transgender identity is hard and can be terrifying at times: ultimately making that first step out the door particularly so. But, over this long process of self discovery and of self acceptance, gradually I had come to a point where I needed to be able to feel free to be out and about and presenting the transgender self. I was still working out what a transgender self looks like but the freedom to be out and wearing a skirt was going to one important element if the battle would ever be won. And I think for me, being out was part of letting go of the shame – hiding in doors reinforces the idea that there is something to be ashamed of.

And being out starts to create new awareness for others, that through a process of familiarisation, a society can become accustomed to difference. Prejudice is invariably born of ignorance and for me there is a point at which the personal is political and I find myself thinking of my gratitude and indebtedness to the tradition we have of civil rights campaigners and social activists – people who were prepared to make a stand to challenge oppression of a disadvantaged group. Through their brave and noble acts others have had greater freedom and I guess it is part of my psychology; part of my philosophy, to take up my responsibility to the cause in a way that honours their value and models an ethic for future generations. I am reminded of a popular quotation – "all that is necessary for evil to triumph is that good men do nothing" (In a slight aside here I would say that this is apparently a misquotation of Edward Burke, the Irish philosopher, who actually wrote:

"when bad men combine, the good must associate; else they will fall one by one, an un-pitied sacrifice in a contemptible struggle". 'from Thoughts on the Cause of present Discontents' 1770.

For me, both quotations have a resonance, but the original carries for me an additional poignancy, the absence of pity perhaps the most significant element in the struggle for transgender recognition as we stand here at the start of the 21st century.

I had already concluded that I was not going to attempt 'passing' as I describe elsewhere in the book, I know that I would not 'pass'. Few do entirely; and being aware of trying, to in a sense 'fool others' into believing I was a natal female would result in a degree of anxiety within me, waiting for the inevitable exposure: I'd be endlessly on my guard. So, lest body language or inner anxiety betrayed the pseudo -representation of a gendered body I chose to be overtly trans – and no mistake. No one fooled, no con.

Although I'd been building up to this day for a very long time, the idea of going outside; in public wearing a skirt and make-up, was anxiety provoking and I wasn't sure just how safe it would be. A few forays in to the garden to experience the feel of wind on a skirt, feel the breeze about the legs had been the limit of my excursions so far – being out in public would be a whole new challenge.

I chose Bristol for my first exploration, I knew the University quarter quite well, it had a good feel, and since I needed to visit the library for more research material an opportunity beckoned.

In planning the look and deciding the outfit I'd decided to make it clear that there was no con – I'm transgender, in a space between male and female and wanted to present that unambiguously (enjoy the paradox). Eddie Izzard does transgender well, blending elements of both genders in a coherent and visually appealing aesthetic: here was my inspiration, a role model so to speak, albeit I have no intention of running marathons or doing stand-up. To that end, I drew together some dynamic elements from the wardrobe. I had thigh high leather stiletto heeled boots, black tights, blue pleated denim miniskirt, blue polo neck jumper, silver jewellery, frock coat and top hat. And eye-make-up; oh, and the beard – yep! As an ensemble it worked well, dramatic, almost gothic, visually it worked although the description here perhaps doesn't do it justice. I drove to Bristol with the accumulated items arranged on the back seat of the car and the make-up in my bag – I was in stealth mode to get out of Wales first.

I arrived in the car park in Bristol. My heart pounding I wrestled with my conscience: did I really want to put myself through this? I weighed it up for what seemed like ages. A part of me wanted to knock the whole idea on the head, chicken out and just go up the library in my jeans and shoes. But, here was my chance, no one knew me here, I could change and just go for it. If I didn't like it I could always return to the car and change back. I weighed it up further. The car park was quiet so I had a go at doing the make-up. A bit of eyeliner, bit of shadow, bit of mascara, not quite the smoky eye effect I was hoping for but I was new to the whole make-up thing and the overall effect was credible enough: task one completed. Now, do I get changed? The question coursed through my mind – I could just do the jeans, coat, hat and make-up – be out as Goth or Emo – it crossed my mind to quit at this stage – it would be easier. A part of me battled this, this was a chance, take a risk, give it a try: gather the data – see it like an experiment. My head buzzing, my heart pounding and my stomach churning I pushed myself and went for it: stood behind the rear door of the car, took my jeans off and slipped on my skirt over the black tights I had on underneath. Task two complete, ok; it's a 'go' - I pulled on the boots, put on the coat and hat, and was ready to roll.

I locked the car and headed for the stairs leading out of the car park. Walking across the concrete of the car park felt strange but ok as I headed past the rows of parked cars towards the door that lead to the stairs. I was now several yards away from the safety of my own car, and outside my comfort zone in both a physical and psychological sense: I was starting to question the whole wisdom of this. I forced myself to push on, concentrating on how I was walking, remembering to keep my back straight, remembering to place one foot in a line in front of the other, heel in front of toe. I'd looked this up on YouTube – how to walk in heels; it was working, I was starting to get a rhythm going, walking from the hips in a motion that is essential to the successful wearing of high heels. And these were high – full-on 4″ stiletto heels, and although I'd sort of practised wearing the boots at home, being out on concrete was a whole new phenomenon but it was ok, it was hanging together. The new sensation of feeling the cool draught of a winter's morning on my legs started to feel good as it gave me the full 'wearing a skirt experience' – something I had been curious about over decades. Now, suddenly, I was doing it, out there, in grrl-mode doing the whole skirt and boots thing. At the door to the stairwell I paused for one final moment before reassuring myself that this would all be fine. Holding the handrail firmly and facing slightly sideways I began the descent. Doing stairs in heels is not for the faint hearted, but I'd done my research and had perfected the ascent and decent of stairs in heels by practising at home, these posed no problem and moments later I was at the exit door of the car park and out on the street leading up to the city centre and university campuses.

A few people milled about, but none posed a problem. I turned left out of the building and headed up the hill towards the shops. A large construction site sat alongside the car park surrounded by tall plywood hoardings. I walked around hoarding using the makeshift footpath, which ran along side, marked out in the road with cones. Reaching the top of the site as I ascended the hill I found the main gates open and a young labourer stood by the large wooden doors, presumably waiting for the next concrete delivery. He caught site of me, and as I walked past in determined strides I heard him call to a colleague and an exchange took place between them. I thought I heard them snigger. I kept walking, confidently, but with a sideways glance in the shop windows to make sure they had not left the site to pursue me. They didn't, and although I'd felt uncomfortable, slightly threatened, it had not been a problem. Making it up to the traffic lights at the top of the hill I stood for a moment to wait for the signal to change. A woman stood along side me, also waiting to cross. We smiled briefly at each other and seconds later the traffic stopped and I was crossing the road in front of a slightly bemused van-driver.

The winter sun gave a clear light and a soft glow of gentle warmth to an otherwise cool November morning as I walked along the row of shops towards the Museum and headed for the route up towards the library. A street seller asked if I wanted to buy a Big Issue. I continued walking on, but a few paces later a pang of remorseful guilt had me turning on my 4" heels and going back to buy a copy. Now, note that this was not an entirely altruistic act I might say, as this also gave me a chance to check his reaction, to gather more data. And yet, the transaction was straightforward and unremarkable, in as much as he seemed completely un-phased by my somewhat exotic array.

Turning left past the street seller on the corner by the museum had me making my way up the steep hill towards the library building. The streets had started to fill with students and commuters heading to work. I smiled at people as I caught their eye: they seemed to smile back if they noticed me. Towards the top of the hill, I was glad to see the university library ahead of me, across the road junction. My feet were really aching, and I was glad to finally make it to the front entrance of the library building. Up the steep hill my mind had entertained itself with Nancy Sinatra singing away on Radio Alex. Her boots may have been made for walking, but these ones weren't – my toes were hurting but hey, ya have to suffer for beauty right?

It had all gone well so far so it seemed ironic that my access to the library would be momentarily delayed by a card fault at the turnstile. A friendly librarian rectified the fault and I soon made it to the top floor to start perusing the shelves.

I took off my coat and hat and piled them with my bag on the seat of a study cubicle. I felt safer here than out in the street. Yes, I felt self-conscious, but kinda knew that people were not in a position to attack me physically or verbally within the university confines. I scanned the shelves and enjoyed the freedom to move about in my boots and skirt. I pulled the sleeves of my jumper above my elbows to expose my forearms – it's a girl thing, bare forearms and by now I was in the habit of keeping them smooth and hairless. I have slender forearms and narrow wrists, these do pass for female, in fact if we are buying bracelets for the darling daughter, it's my wrist that is the best match to check for a fit. Yeah, weird.

I enjoyed a few hours there, making notes and getting references for the thesis. Eventually it was time to go, and now I find that heading down the hill back into the town centre was presenting a whole new challenge. Walking down a steep hill in 4" stiletto heels had not been covered in any of the YouTube training videos – I hadn't factored this one in and neither had I checked out the protocol on walking in heels on cobbles. It felt precarious and I was concerned about falling, I was concerned about failing – I would lose credibility if I ended up in a heap on the floor. I doubled my concentration, blocked my mind to the pain in my toes as they pushed even harder into the point of the boots and focussed back on the routine – one foot in front of the other, heel in front of toe, walk from the hips, keep the back straight, the head looking up. Cobble was soon again replaced by paving slab – and the trick here was to avoid the cracks in the pavement – not because the bears would jump out and eat me, nope, I needed to be fearful of the horrible pavement trolls lest they grab the tip of one of my heels and snap it off to make delicious troll-stew: I was careful let me tell you.

Towards the bottom of the hill a bin lorry was at work, a couple of lads in yellow visi-jackets worked their way up the street in front of me, grabbing bins and hauling them towards the rear of the truck. I started to panic – was this safe, how would they react, was there another route to take to avoid them. The thoughts pounded through my brain. Once again I fought the battle between the part of me that thought it was stupid to put myself through this and the part of me that wanted to be out, to overcome the prejudice – mine and societies. I contemplated turning back, finding an escape route, I considered crossing the street but that felt like the coward's thing to do, and that might even bring more attention so I decided to brave it out and keep going, straight past them. As I reached the rear of the lorry I looked in the eye of one of the bin-men, and with a slight nod and semi smile towards him carried on. Unlike the labourers there was no comment. It had not been a problem. A sense of relief passed through me but by now I was tired and weary: I had really pushed myself, taken the courage to be out and I was pleased to have done it but my feet were killing me, my head was hurting and I just wanted to be back in the car park and sitting within the sanctuary of the car; heading home. The large construction site lay ahead but I was beyond caring, I would be on the opposite side of the road anyway and would adopt the nonchalant attitude I had used past the bin men to avoid aggro. As it turned out, the route back proved uneventful.

Finding myself once more in the car park and stood by the side of the car I was soon kicking off my heels and slipping into something more comfortable. I felt a sense of achievement and albeit it had been scary I'd been ok. The situations I'd encountered had been perfectly manageable, it was all about positive mental attitude. It was time to head home but, enjoying the new freedom of being out, I kept the skirt on and drove most of the way home before finding a quiet lay-by to get changed back into trousers and remove the make-up.

It was however, several months before another opportunity to go out presented itself.

Eddie Izzard – Actor, Comedian,

T-girl

I went to see the Doctor wearing make-up:

Izzard: 'I've got a cough'

Doctor: 'You've got what?'

Izzard: 'I've got a cough.'

Doctor: 'You're a transvestite?'

Izzard: 'No. I've got a cough. I am a transvestite, but I've got a cough.'

Doctor: 'Well, I'd better sort the transvestite thing out. Have to refer you for that'

Izzard: 'No, that's not a problem. Just the cough thanks.'

(Izzard et al. 1998: p63)

How am I looking?

I'm sitting on a train: it's late, and I'm on my way back from a long day in London - but I'm feeling good; energised. The headache of earlier has shifted and I am knocking through a book on gender studies and feminist theory, impatiently reading it with a combination of fascination and curiosity. My 'passenger services host' tells me through his scratchy tannoy that the buffet car, "located between coaches F and E in the middle of the train is now open for refreshments": which is nice to know. And actually, a cup of complimentary coffee (a privilege of first class) could be just the thing. I decide to make the excursion, leaving my bag and jacket on the seat as it seems quiet, but taking my phone and wallet just in case, and my top hat.

The coach is almost empty, and I am unnoticed as I stand up and straighten and smooth the pleats of my denim mini skirt. I would say here that it's kinda cute as skirts go, fifteen inch from waist to hem, it moves and hangs well, the box pleats giving it fullness and shape. My friend Tina couldn't believe that I'd actually made it myself - she said it looked amazing but I'm aware of the flaws in my stitching,,. maybe in a way that carries personal symbolism. But I love it, not least because it actually fits: Annoyingly, I've got the classic snake hips and no bum that makes getting a skirt or dress to hang nicely, nigh on impossible.

I remember an article in Cosmo that said how easy it is as a girl to focus on the parts of our bodies we don't like. Focus instead it suggests, on the bits you do like and make the most of them - I think I have nice eyes, and today I'm really pleased with the 'classic smoky eye effect' I created with my new Clinique pony-tail smudge brush (it's so important to have the right tools for a job I find). That, and some notes I made from a tutorial on YouTube, which showed you how, in easy step-by-step stages. I should explain that I'd kind of missed out on the whole learning about make-up thing when I was younger - it has to be said that my mother certainly didn't approve so I never got the chance to experiment. Thank goodness for YouTube. In fact, thank goodness for the Internet, it's an ideal place for a girl like me to learn the things I missed out on or never knew.

I move through the carriages of the train towards the buffet. In coach F are some Cardiff City fans drinking lager. It's a concern. There's a rowdiness evident and for a moment I wonder about turning back. They are in first class though; maybe this is a better class of football hooligan - maybe I mis-judge them; stereotypes are so destructive. I decide to brave it out but my optimism starts to seem misplaced.

"Oi: Boy George", shouts one of the group as he spots me.

I'm walking steadily past them, ignoring the comment. I suddenly feel something brush the hem of my skirt, a hand reaching under,

"Skirt: here you are, sit on my dick."

It's not an offer I'm inclined to give consideration to. The last of the group has his leg across the gangway and momentarily distracted by what just occurred, I inadvertently kick it as I try to step over him. This is not a good plan and I'm starting to regret a lot of things - not least of which was dismissing the thought to change into my jeans once I'd got on the train. I give him eye contact and a 'sorry mate' and he seems ok with that. I move through the automated sliding door and thankfully I find myself in the sanctuary of the buffet car.

Two Asian girls in traditional dress are picking up their order and putting the change away: I'm not sure if they have noticed me, they avoid giving me eye contact. The attendant standing behind the counter looks up and greets me with a warm smile. Now in a position to attach a visual image to the scratchy tannoyed voice who told me he was my 'passenger services host' I establish what one actually looks like: In this case, he reminds me of Marc Almand of 80's pop group 'Soft Cell' - only with a quiff. His small frame and soft young face perform a gender that somehow sits between biological binaries and I read him as slightly effeminate, may be even gay. Not in an overt campy way but you understand, more in a soft, gentle way that tells me he is clearly not a 'PROPER MAN'. I ask for a coffee; just black coffee thanks. He places the cup in a dinky little paper carrier bag and I contemplate my return.

The thought of the Cardiff football fans now concerns me. Maybe I should just stay at this end of the train until the end of the journey. DAMN; left my bag and my jacket at the other end; I just can't leave it. I've got to go back; I conjure with metaphors - back through the 'lions den' or is that 'gorilla pit'. For a moment

I consider asking the guard who has joined my 'passenger services host' if he could accompany me down the train to keep order (protect me) but decide to tough it out 'like a MAN'. As I re-enter the carriage the lads eyeball me and the loudest one starts the chant -

"Karma, karma karma karma karma chameleon: Oi, Boy George"

The boys chorus together, chanting the first line repeatedly, throwing in the odd 'Oi Boy George' for lyrical effect until it begins to take on the form of some avant-garde fugue you'd find created by music college undergraduates. I fear this is not the case sadly, these Neanderthals simply lack the intelligence or wit to know any more of the song. A pity really as the irony of their choice of song is also lost on them. When Boy George wrote the song he was encouraging people to be true to the self; have the courage of your conviction, he was telling people; to express their true selves rather than always trying to blend in with the crowd - changing their colours to suit the environment: he says being false to the self leaves bad karma. That's all very well for him to say but I'm on a train with a load of soccer thugs wondering if I'm about to pay some karmic price for trying to be myself.

The lad who invited me to 'sit on his dick' has possibly worked out the paradox of his request - in front of his friends he did just ask a bloke to sit on his penis and since I'm not the one with the homosexual desires it places him in an awkward imbroglio. He remedies this by clarifying - "it's got a beard". The "it's" is emphasised:- a kind of verbal rubric.

Yeah; well done Captain Observant of the Sharp Eyed People - albeit I'm wearing a skirt I think you'll find we carry the same chromosomal format XY: but does that make me just like you - a 'guy' a 'geezer' a 'bloke' a 'MAN'? I mean, how can one know; how to decide; what you do you read - the skirt or the beard. Some kind of primeval mechanism was moving through his reptilian brain (by which I mean the amygdala in case you think I'm just being nasty now) assessing 'do I fuck it or fight it?' Actually dear boy, perhaps we can do neither. I'd quite like to just go back to my carriage and drink my coffee and read my book.

The lads are chanting still, but an internal dialogue is taking over which is louder - a steady reassuring voice that calms me. I avoid eye contact and continue with faux-nonchalance, my heart is pounding; my ears hyper-vigilant to the possible sound of footsteps behind me. I reach the door at the end of carriage F and wait an eternity for the automated door mechanism to open. Finally, the door slides to the left and I make a silent sigh of relief and pass through, returning now to the relative safety of my carriage, my table, my seat.

I'm annoyed: annoyed with myself for putting me through that; annoyed that others are like that.   I'm annoyed at men; at faux masculinity and the sexual aggressiveness. I'm annoyed at Football, the locus of so much destructive masculine identity. I'm annoyed at the memories of being terrified in the playground by lads like that. And at a life lived in stealth, endlessly trying to 'pass' as a boy, as a guy, as a MAN.

My inner voice has calmed me, and congratulated me on handling things really well in a way I never had at school; at home. I'm proud of myself: that I didn't over-react or run scared. I wonder if now is the time to change into my jeans - but no, damn it: I determine to wait until I reach Newport before I change. I smile and reflect on the thoughts and memories of my day 'out'.

London was amazing. I'm walking through the centre of London, almost invisible. I start to feel like the Matt Lucas character from Llanddewi Brefi - no one seems to have noticed. "Excuse me - I am transgender you know, gender-queer. I like girls but I like dressing like one too." The voice in my head (which took on a west Wales lilt for added effect) has narrated it silently to the passers-by who seem un-phased; yeah; whatever. Children are brilliant - their reactions, the double take. A girl of four or five at the museum has paused to look at me, and like an anchor that halts the giant ship as it catches something misshapen on the sea bed, her tiny hand has gripped her father's and halted him: stopped him in his tracks.

"I like the man's pink boots"

I smile at her and look over at her parents; the mother adds, "and she was admiring your purple scarf too". Perhaps there's a hesitation in her voice, uncertainty mixed with warmth but maybe somehow lacking the innocent honesty of her daughter's tone.

"That girl's got good taste" I quip as I walk on, smiling; amused.

But then it has to be said my pink fury Ugg boots are well lush and the purple mohair scarf set against the black leather biker jacket and top hat create quite an ensemble if I do say so myself: that, and the pleated denim mini-skirt of course. I'm wearing black woolly tights today, which I have chosen to balance the dark polo neck jumper. And being January I'd prepared for cold weather of course.

I return to reading my book, and the world is at peace. I am at peace.

Time passes slowly on the train but I'm making good progress with the book when my attention is taken by the arrival of two of the soccer rowdies in my carriage. Their coarse language, rumbustious physicality and loud tone perform a hegemonic masculinity that tells the world they are real MEN. They stop at a table further up the carriage but their presence can be felt from where I am sitting and I conclude it is time to quickly change back in to my jeans, a task I can achieve from under the table without being noticed. Their conversation is animated as they discuss football, arguments between the group, and the importance they place on being able to engage in a relaxing activity at the weekend after a hard week's work and not have to deal with the aggro. So, maybe we are very much alike. Constrained to a role; meeting the demands of others, these guys have dressed up for a day's relaxation. I wonder if they think of their football shirts as a form of drag - which of course it is, intrinsically serving the same purpose: identification, belonging, escapism, relaxation.

The train arrives at Newport and I step onto the platform. It's quiet but then it's late: two Police officers are on duty and I catch the eye and smile at the WPC. I walk towards the exit and notice a young woman emerging at pace through the main doors. She has the most amazing purple hair, and tights to match: I read her as a kindred soul, a bohemian, she's no karma chameleon. She looks up at and smiles at me,

"Hmm, I'm liking.." she says, turning her head for an extended gaze as she passes me.

She's read my top hat, my scarf, my biker jacket, my skinny black jeans, my pink furry boots; the smoky eyes. For a moment we share a connection; the artistic; creative; the expression of the self against convention. I think she'd have loved the pleated denim mini skirt too. I'm almost sorry I don't still have it on. I feel a desire to reciprocate - to validate her, for having the courage of her conviction, but the moment has passed. I've not commended her on the purple hair, which I'm liking but it's too late. A slight sadness and regret passes through me.

Outside the air is cool and the streets quiet. The car is barely quarter of a mile away and the decision is whether to take a taxi or chance going though the underpass and just walk. I go for it, it seems quiet and in the underpass I follow behind a guy who seems reasonable; I'm walking more quickly so I pass him and walk ahead. I'm counting the steps like seconds ticking, each drawing me closer to the exit, back to the safety of the car. I'm nearing the end of the underpass when from around the corner I hear voices and my heart skips for a moment. A middle-aged couple return from a night on the town - the woman is pulling up her tights in a somewhat undignified manner. In my head I say to her, "cheap tights yeah; what a nightmare, tell me about it - I prefer M&S myself". I resist the temptation and merely smile at her and wink. She smiles back - I don't think she knows I'm wearing tights too.

Emerging from the underpass and turning the corner I make the short walk up the hill to the safety of the car. It's been a long day but a good one.

64   Doing Transgender

Kinky Boots (2005)

Miramax

Actors: Joel Edgerton as Charlie Price, Chiwetel Ejiofor as Lola/Simon, Sarah-Jane Potts as Lauren

Director: Julian Jarrold

DVD Timing: 0:25:30

Lauren: We don't have many transvestites in Northampton.

Lola: I'm not merely a transvestite, sweetheart. I'm also a drag queen. It's a simple equation. A drag queen puts on a frock, looks like Kylie. A transvestite puts on a frock, looks like… Boris Yeltsin in lipstick. There, I said it. (*Charlie hands him a drink*) Ta. Whatever. Don't kid yourself. You're never more than ten feet away from a transvestite

Mr Ben.

Back in the 1970's television was simple. The Clangers - stuffed socks that whistled to each other and lived on the moon with a soup dragon; The Flower Pot Men – two guys who played in the potting shed with their friend 'Weed' (nice one – that sure ducked the radar), and a beardy wierdy Canadian called Yoffy who sat at a wooden kitchen table with some glove puppets and gave us Fingerbobs. In all fairness I remember these with great affection, it was an innocent time for television. We didn't question things in those days, everything was taken at face value. Of course, as a forty something academic in the cynical 21st century what better occupation than exploring the subtext to these subversive political offerings clothed as children's light entertainment. (Mind you I look forward to the dissertations exploring the psychodynamics of the character of Stephanie from Lazy Town – an 18 year old woman playing the part of a coquettish 8 year old in a program designed to brain wash children into thinking that the sharp tasting acidic and unripe fruit we buy in this country is actually 'candy' – purlease.). Meanwhile, back to the innocent comfort of the 1970's.

And here, against this backdrop of simple but charming children's characters, an artist and writer called David McKee launched onto an unsuspectingly naive and unquestioning public a curious but apparently innocent protagonist in the form of Mr Ben. The story is a simple one. A man in a suit and a bowler hat, carrying a briefcase, leaves his house at 52 Festive Road in the morning. He looks very much like any city chap off to work in the banking industry or civil service. So we watch him as he walks down the road as if heading off to work but this guy has a secret, for he has no intention of getting on the tube and going to work – today he will indulge a hidden passion, a kink for dressing up. He has found himself on the high street at the fancy dress shop. He's clearly a regular here as the shop keeper easily recognises him. 'Good Morning sir, what will it be today? It's not long before our protagonist has taken his chosen costume into the changing room, and is hurriedly getting changed into it. It seems only a moment before the costume change is complete and he is able to gaze at himself in the full length mirror.

Here, as he gazes at himself in the clothes he is now wearing he enters a fantasy world where he lives out the dream life symbolised by his costume – be it native American, spaceman, circus clown et al. Strangely, he never did ballerina or bride or French-maid, which I think is a shame. Still, seeing as they cancelled the translation to screen of his book 123456Ben, about him being in prison, perhaps an overtly transvestite storyline would be too avant-garde: this is the 1970's remember.

Now, I would argue that in many ways this was a classic cross-dressing narrative. He presents a false but acceptable self to the world – ask yourself for a moment why it was that he left the house dressed as if for work. If this was his day off we might expect him in jeans and jumper to go down the shops. I think the suit; bowler hat and briefcase are significant here as it retains the illusion of a cover story – a respectable false self to be observed by the neighbours. Here he presents (passes) as respectable, authoritative, important. A more cynical observer might suggest the possibility that he had been made redundant but couldn't live with the shame so makes out he is going to work and then spends the day in the fancy dress shop rather than attending the job seekers club down at the local labour exchange.

Interestingly too, we might note that despite the raging heteronormativity of the 1970's, and especially 1970's television, there is strangely no mention of a wife: no loving and dutiful wife to kiss good-bye before going into town – a significant omission I'd say.

So here's my hypothesis: Mr Ben is a tranny! Let me explain - when I was a boy (in the 1960's/1970's) dressing up – indeed liking dressing up was definitely classed as girly or poofy as soon as you were old enough to know that being girly or poofy was a bad thing (so work on about being five for that). So, a grown man who likes dressing up and spending ages gazing at himself in the mirror having a fantasy about the costume and the magical effect it has on his psyche - come on – this guy is a 'tranny' and no mistake. If you have yet to be convinced I might invite you to further consider why was it necessary to have a middle aged man to live out this role – the story could quite easily have been of a young boy who would go on a Saturday to find a kindly old shop keeper who would let him play in the stock room. Now that would have plausibility but no, this is darker in a way that warrants consideration from a queer perspective. No money changes hands – which we'd forgive if a child came to play. This middle-aged man comes into a costume shop, takes a costume into the changing room, spends a while gazing at himself in the mirror wearing the costume (and imagines what it is like to wear this costume full time/ to be this person – in what could perhaps be described as a psychic onanistic fantasy) then simply hands back the costume to the shop keeper since he had no intention of taking it out on hire and or paying for it. Try doing that at your local costume hire shop (or for a real challenge try something a bit more fun like Pronuptia) and I think you'll find they give you short shrift.

So, it's drag – the adoption of a costume and an identity defined by clothes. In each episode he got to do something for the greater good – in some way his intervention in the world of the fantasy was beneficial to them so he gets a feel good factor (perhaps to mitigate his guilt at the cross-dressing) and of course he is left with some legacy memento of each adventure. Here I like the double-entendre. For the cross-dresser there is always the fear of discovery by a legacy memento – the piece of clothing left out or put back incorrectly, a piece of jewellery or trace of make-up that betrays the secret. Here, his mementos are played as positive reminders – like the transgender male who goes to the dressing house and has photographs taken – flicking through the album and remembering the adventure -this is when I was a bridesmaid, a bride, a fairy, a ballerina, a French maid, a school girl.

I've had my own Mr Ben moments too – like now, writing this on the late train back to South Wales. I've had a great weekend in London and enjoyed two whole days being 'out and proud' in trans mode, doing T-grrl. And although today as I come home from my adventure, I have had to change back into my jeans I have my legacy memento – this time I have brought back a picture of Camden Market as a reminder of a place where alternative is normal, and drab is the outsider. I shall hang it in my room as a reminder of my adventure.

1995: 'To Wong Foo, Thanks For Everything: Julie Newmar',

Universal Picturees

Video timing: (0:25:18)

Chi-Chi (Leguizmo) "What d'ya mean, 'be' a Drag Queen, I am a Drag Queen"

Noxeema (Snipes) "Oh, child, no,no,no: You simply a boy put in a dress. When a straight man puts on a dress and gets his sexual kicks: He is a transvestite. When a man is a woman trapped in a man's body and he has a little operation: He is a transsexual"

Chi-Chi (Leguizmo) "I know that"

Noxeema (Snipes) "When a gay man has way too much fashion sense for just one gender: HE is a drag queen"

Vida (Swayzee) "Thank you"

Noxeema: (Snipes) "And when a tired little Latin boy puts on a dress, he is simply, a boy in a dress"

Featuring: Wesley Snipes: Noxeema; Patrick Swayze: Vida; John Leguizmo: Chi-Chi; Stockard Channing: Carole-Ann

That's a Laydee!

Let's face it – we've all seen one. And I think this is part of the problem.

In 2007 the actor and comedian David Walliams famously presented his transvestite character to the world with the catch phrase –'I'm a laydee'. He and Matt Lucas offered us a vision of the self-deceiving transvestite. We're invited to believe that these two see themselves as 'passing', as being 'read' and received as female, as 'Laydees' yet the joke in this case is clearly on them – they fool no-one. The characters represent, in artistic terms the classic comedic grotesque: but what is Walliams saying in this parody of the transgender male? Consideration of the word grotesque is a useful starting point – reference to the dictionary sees it described as odd, unnatural in shape, appearance or character; fantastically ugly or absurd; bizarre. Kinda sums it up yeah?

"My name is Emily Howard and I'm a laydee and I like doing ladies things like knitting and crochet and playing with little kittens".

The false/falsetto voice; crudely applied and excessive make-up; the Edwardian frilled dress; the awkward body movements, all combine to create a discordant symphony to betray the attempted deception. The musical analogy would perhaps best describe this performance as being played with the naivety and inexperience of a primary school orchestra: the notes are there but somehow in the wrong places, landing uncomfortably: it jars. The audience recognise the tune and applaud politely but we know they've heard and noted the discrepancies; they set these aside, here there's a forgiveness; a collusion to create an alternative reality – "wow, weren't they amazing". Like transvestites in a meeting house "wow darling, you can pass really convincingly" "Thanks Dave, sorry - Diana."

I'm being bitchy I know, ([sic] ooh, just like a 'real girl') but I think my disquiet here is that in the case of music, when intelligently done, the rules can be transcended; queered, played with; to create new and innovative. This is in contrast to those times when we hear a familiar tune played crudely, naively or lacking the subtleties of nuance and tone- it just ain't right and it ain't clever enough to call itself jazz. And this might offer an interesting paradigm to explore further. A monkey let loose in an orchestra pit does not create jazz by bashing instruments randomly (although this might be my submission for next year's Turner prize – I'm liking the idea). No, the jazz musician understands the rules of music precisely, and in properly understanding the rules he thus knows how to break them. Emily Howard, the crap transvestite is discordant, clumsy, grating to the senses. So the challenge is how to avoid the discordant and grating – the grotesque, and aim for an off-beat improvised riff, a gendered melody that might wilfully and overtly break the conventions of a strict 4/4 time or 8 note scale yet still emerge as groovy nonetheless. And hey, not everyone likes Jazz, not everyone understands Jazz but it still works – can transgender?

So how to apply the paradigm – (ok, albeit with apologies to all those hard working primary school music co-ordinators who are deeply offended – sorry guys) how might the contrasting of primary school orchestra and jazz musician teach us something about being and presenting (or indeed 'performing' to use Butler's term) Transgender?

There's something rather organic and organismic about music. Music seems to have an intrinsic rightness abut it and we know when it's not right. Is this the problem with transgender? Does it break a fundamental piece of hardwired programming? I'm ambivalent about that one. Jazz improvisation breaks the rules of notated music but still has some fundamental structure underneath it. What is it about sex and gender that is so deeply ingrained; what is it that makes a 'tranny' so easy to spot at fifty paces?

I might revisit briefly a theme covered in an earlier chapter – the primal 'fuck it or fight it' theory. From the human as reproductive animal perspective I guess it's useful to know how to read someone. And maybe we are programmed to spot discrepancy – deception too. Let's face it Walliams' character sits like a pantomime dame on a bus -the presentation of an overly and overtly performative femme-self, visual rubrics – ruffles, excessive make-up. Shouting loudly to the world – I AM a laydee. The need to shout acting as proof of the counter-point: he doth protest too much. But do we have to shout, can transgender be played more softly, a quite hum to the self rather than operatic rendition to the attendant audience. In my own journey I think I recognise that I have moved from wanting acknowledgement as a 'girl', see me as a girl, treat me as a girl (what ever that is) to accepting that people will still refer to me as 'Sir' but I have nonetheless communicated a girl-ness to them. I have distinguished myself from hegemonic masculinity sufficiently to have made the point. From a positioning of self that was looking to see how others receive me (am I ok) to just being, getting on and doing anyway.

My journey has been about finding how to do a transgender self that is honest – not 'passing' but being. If I'm out in 'Grrl-mode' do I have to wear a skirt? Obviously when the opportunity arises I'm keen to make the most of it, but do I have to always, what, just to prove the bloody point? Sometimes it seems like there are few opportunities to do so that perhaps it feels like I'm missing out if I just do jeans. It's a struggle to know.

So, today I'm out – an excursion to London for a conference. And I'm in jeans – so that's not very girly is it? I've got my black Uggs, my skinny jeans; my pink scarf and pink leopard print belt; my waistcoat; my jewellery. I've got hair today – it's a straight wig (a concession to male pattern baldness), and a silver hair-band. And a little make-up: light foundation to hide some of the effects of age; and eyeliner and mascara set off with just a little shadow to blend it at the edges. It's quite minimal for me – I'm a real sucker for the smoky-eye look. (Did I hear someone say Panda eyes? – Harsh girlfriend, wash your mouth out with soap and fetch yourself a saucer of milk – meow).

So, there are overt signs of girl self – the visual codes – long hair, silver hair-band, pink; signs of an alternative gender presentation and Goth and Emo elements – the silver jewellery; the eyeliner; these could be read as Goth/Emo. I get on the train at Tottenham Court Road to take the northern line to Camden. As the carriages pulled along I scanned quickly for a safe carriage to join – a flash of pink caught my eye. A middle-aged woman was seated in the carriage at the end, with a teenage girl stood next to her. Both had punky spiked hair with pink flashes in it. The girl had a lush pair of pink furry leg-shields. These were clearly my kind of people. I got on and there was a smile of mutual acknowledgement. We didn't speak.

I scanned the carriage – although relatively full no one seemed bothered by my presence, no one posed overt threat. I scanned to see who might give eye contact acknowledgment. All quiet on the western front. The punky girl had a brief conversation in German with a man stood next to her and I guessed this guy, albeit a bit more conservative in dress was most likely her father.

As the carriage rattled along the northern line, heading for Warren Street, a carriage full of bored zombie like beings sat in silence, enclosed in a personal bubble that acted like an invisible protective force field around them: - for some their comfort zone reinforced by the additional protective shield of iPod ear piece or mobile phone screen. Suddenly my eye was drawn to a fantastic exchange through the medium of sign language that was passing between mother and daughter – a powerful sort of library silence – odd words mouthed, partial sounds, rapid movements of hands and fingers to create the dialogue between them. I loved the joy that existed between them – this girl seemed to be held with pride and affection by her parents.

As we drew into Camden and I made for the door it didn't surprise me that they were getting off at this stop too. We followed each other up the long staircase towards the exit, and then finally, as I passed my ticket through the exit machine and pushed my way past the turnstile, I looked over my shoulder for a moment, to pass them a final acknowledgement, a fond farewell and in doing so caught the eye of the woman - and yes, there was a brief yet silent acknowledgement of that shared queering of social norms, a look, a smile, an affirmation to each other.

Walking around Camden market with the beautiful people felt good. In this bohemian enclave the plain and drab are the strangers; the ones who become 'other'. Here I find myself able to relax, be comfortable in my identity and enjoy the freedom. Camden market is such an exotic place and with strong Goth and Emo influences, I fit in easily. I wander around the market place, visit the stalls, treat myself to a T-shirt that proclaims "Nobody knows I'm a lesbian", and a photo-on-canvas picture of Camden high street to frame and hang in my room back home. Time passes quickly here, there is so much to see, so much to experience and take in: suddenly I notice the time, it's mid-day, so I buy some lunch from a Thai curry stall, munch it down quick before heading back to the tube station and making it across town to attend a workshop on Sexuality, the main reason this time for trekking into London.

I arrive at the conference and feel at ease among the group. I'm aware of wearing make-up and the wig and hair band but it's a look that hangs together, the visual aesthetic works and people are warm towards me. That evening, I grab some dinner in a quiet restaurant before making it back on the underground to the hotel. Today is the first time I've worn this wig out in public and I've been aware of feeling unsure about how it will be received, the impact on people's reaction. Although it was relatively cheap it suits me and it doesn't look too odd – it's not so different to how my hair was before it got too thin and fell out.

I arrive in the hotel and unpack my outfit for tomorrow. I have packed a favourite skirt which is getting an outing this time. Now, part of the whole girl thing is you end up having to remember what you wore last time so as not to always be out in the same thing, to remember to choose a different outfit each time. I've done the denim, pleated mini-skirt twice here, so this time I've brought the blue box-pleat. I pull it out of the bag and am disgruntled to find it creased. A pang of sadness and disappointment passes through me as I contemplate giving it a miss and just wearing the jeans again tomorrow. Not one to give up easily, I decide to see if I can engineer a solution to the problem. Assessing the available resources I figure I can lift the lid off the kettle, boil up some steam, steam out the creases and leave it hanging over the radiator. It's worth a shot and sure enough, first thing in the morning, as if by magic it is as good as new, pleats sharp as ever, creases gone. Magic! I get dressed and go up to the breakfast room in my skirt and boots, wearing make-up and jewellery, the wig and the hair band. It's still early days for me being out and I've needed to give myself a prep talk before walking out of the door. The dining room is busy and I am crammed onto a small table where I am one of the few diners breakfasting alone. I think the feeling is something akin to jumping in the school swimming pool when you are a kid. There is a dread – it will be uncomfortable at first but you figure once you are in it will be ok. This is the same, and after a few minutes to acclimatise I start to feel ok. I smile at the waitress – she's Polish or Ukrainian I think and I order some toast and black coffee. I feel ok; it's slightly weird but I'm ok and I'm out, doing transgender.

Breakfast completed, I check out of the hotel and enjoy the walk to the train station, moving my body in feminine ways, and feeling confident; feeling content.

As I travel across town I start to focus less on how people might be seeing me and just enjoy being me. It's an interesting shift from the anxious self-consciousness that draws attention, to a position of inner confidence that becomes more invisible. Arriving at the conference for the second day and I am greeted warmly once again and there are compliments about how my outfit works well. It is where I have figured I needed to be, finding outfits that would fit properly; hang properly; co-ordinate properly and ultimately present well. This skirt is a classic stitched down box pleat in navy blue which I tailored in at the hips to get it to hang better and this means I don't need hip pads underneath it. The stitched down pleating at the top of the skirt fits my hips and allows the pleats to flare out nicely. I always wanted one like this, and here I am spending the day in it. As the day progresses and I get on with the business of the conference I become less conscious of wearing the skirt and it just starts to feel totally natural to the point where I forget and wonder why I could feel the breeze about my legs and then remember – I'm wearing a skirt, in public, out – 'Jinkies!' The thought still feels odd and I think about the progression from stealing secret and fleeting moments where I could try one on, to trying one on briefly in the privacy of my home, to a point where not only can I wear one out, I can forget I'm actually wearing one. It just feels natural. And that is a really comfortable feeling, the tension and anxiety are gone – and that feels good.

So, a colleague has asked a favour, a big one. Now, I don't like having my picture taken normally but there's something different about being 'out' in grrl-mode – perhaps a record or memento, a reminder, and to some degree a reality check – the viewing of the self through a photograph is different to the mirror. It's a more objective look I think. So, I have agreed to pose outside the fruit and veg shop on the high street to pose a shot. My colleague wants to have an example of someone with a more integrated and coherent trans look. I'm encouraged (I guess I struggle to admit being flattered – maybe I am a bit flattered) and the photo is credible although it's interesting that viewed from behind the stance is still male. I think it's in the way the arms hang. It reminds me why 'passing' is such a difficult and elusive thing – there are so many clues indicating the nature of the individual's natal and chromosomal sex. Anyway, the look hangs together and I'm quite pleased. My friend remarks – "spot the fruit" – Droll!

We return to the conference and enjoy an exciting and challenging afternoon. My queer friends have liked my look and there was a lot of affirmation. Two of the guys have complimented me on the skirt – there is a longing within them to be able to do the same it seems but they too are fearful. I am touched by the acceptance and warmth and wish I could find the same level of acceptance in my primary social network. I explain to them that I don't feel able to go into the local village like this for fear of intolerance and abuse. As the meeting draws to a close this reality hits home – it's back to South Wales tonight: and suddenly I feel the sadness and disappointment of seeing my excursion drawing to a close. I am strangely reminded of the children's television series of Mr Ben and find myself for a moment feeling a childhood empathy with him - for that penultimate moment when 'as if by magic the shop keeper would appear' and beckon him –'this way sir' back to his drab (Dressed As A Boy-DRAB consider the play on words here) life, back to the constraint of the black suit and bowler hat and the conservative folk of Festive Road.

Still before my day is done I have a couple of hours left in London to trek across town on the tube and get some dinner before the long train journey home.

Now, I have a favourite restaurant in London – it's Persian and just up the road from the station at Paddington. I stumbled across it the first time I did the girl thing and was looking for somewhere quiet where I could eat a reasonably priced meal in peace without aggro. The proprietor looks extraordinarily like Corporal Klinger from Mash (so think of the irony here as he of course is not the one apparently in drag). He's a great guy and now I've been there a few times he's got to know me and the welcome is always really warm and welcoming. I think I'm pleasantly surprised as maybe I thought he'd have cultural injunctions against queerness – clearly not, so that would be my prejudice. This has been an important piece of learning for me as I explore a queer identity and go out as trans. The prejudice sometimes sits within me – the fear of discrimination or of hostility or threat is my fantasy rather than a reality. I have been aware of an increasing confidence and assuredness being out which means I can feel less vulnerable, less threatened. It always does however come back to clusters of the low intelligence ill educated boy/men who see queer as a threat and threaten back. And this is no different for the typical single girl – maybe this is the reality of the 'real girl' experience, feeling vulnerable to verbal or indeed physical assault from low intelligence, ill educated boy/men. Either way, I figure I'm going to have to change into my trousers before we hit Newport – it's just too risky. It might be interesting to try eye make-up in Newport with jeans and boots and see what reactions that gets – but that's for another day.

I enjoy my meal and make it back to the station in perfect time to board the train. It seems surprisingly busy tonight, most of the seats occupied and I'm relieved to have escaped any harassing comments or aggro this time. I always travel first class when doing the girl thing – the clientele in first class seem safer. There was a gang of 'lads' that went up the carriage in raucous and slightly menacing way but thankfully I was in a forward facing seat so they didn't clock me. They were headed for the standard class carriages further up the train.

With the journey back to South Wales well under way I contemplate getting a cup of coffee from the buffet car. I pull my jeans out of the overnight bag and head to the toilet compartment to get changed. Working my way up the carriage towards the end I pass a few rows of bored business types before I come across a group of middle-aged women clearly having a party at the head of the coach. They are in playful mood – they have champagne and chocolates and it looks like they've had a girlie outing to London (well me too!). I smile at them and remark that they know how to travel in style. They laugh and one comments that she digs the skirt, another remarks that she had one exactly like that in school. I simply quip back to them,

"Ah, yeah, you can't beat a classic box pleat!"

and then I pass through the door to the lobby of the train carriage and into the toilet where I get changed into my jeans: but feeling in buoyant mood leave the hair and make-up to take off when I'm back home.

It's been an interesting couple of days, I've learned a lot, personally and professionally, it's been a good trip.

Pride And Prejudice

I'm driving to Newport and I am re-affirming myself with a positive mindset. It's the first time I've done a transgender look in Newport and I've been working up to this one. I've felt somehow uncomfortable with the idea up to now – Newport has felt too rough, too weighted towards the kinds of people [boys] that made my life hell in school, who were intolerant, who wanted to attack non-conformity. And although I have come to challenge some of my hyper-vigilance – the perception of all places 'out there' as dangerous - to realise that there are more places where I can be out and where people can accept me, just leave me alone, or ignore me, (I'm not fussy which) I have to wrestle with the times when there seems like evidence is there to back up the fear that it might be too dangerous, where I might be attacked. And I reflect on the difference between my process and the experience of a 'real girl': does a lone female walk through an underpass at night or fear assault; what does it feel like for a woman to have to walk past a group of men – particularly say builders, scaffolders and the like – is it safe, scary, unsettling? If I am to openly inhabit some of the space defined as female then perhaps the reality is that the threat of assault and assaulting comment by ill-educated and low intelligence males is part of the 'real girl' experience.

Anyway, I've played a bit safe today so I am not in a skirt – more than anything this seems to be the thing that breaks the rules most. So today I have long hair and eye make-up; I've got my skinny black jeans and my black ankle boots with the pointed toe and step heel. And today I'm wearing feather earrings, a Goth coat and my silver jewellery – it's a queer look, with gothic influences and I am content with it, it feels congruent, it feels like me. I determine to factor in a visit to Blue Banana: I love Blue Banana, it's a Gothy/Emo themed shop and I adore so many of the clothes in it, particularly the gothic-lolita styled dresses which are just so cute, so uber-girly and so totally not going to look good on my body. Damn it 'Just like a real girl' – I endlessly experience the frustration of my body-shape not suiting the clothes I'd love to wear. Anyway, back to the story. Heading for Newport I have a plan - I have a favourite car-park, close to the town which will afford me a swift route in.

Now, as I've remarked before, Robert Burns the Scots poet accurately observed that the best laid plans of mice and men oft go awry and today is proof of this one. Arriving in Newport I am distressed to find my 'safe' car park is full so I now have to travel to a further one – and this will mean a longer walk: suddenly a degree of anxiety and annoyance passes through me. Why do I push myself to do this, have I put myself in danger? I settle myself, drive up the road and pull into another car park and find a space. The ticket machine is broken and I notice my frustration and anxiety build – now more than ever the thought to go home and give up pounds the back of my head, but keeping myself grounded, I just call the phone number of the park attendant from the safety of my car. Surprisingly the phone is answered, the guy knows there's a problem but it's ok, I can park for free. I prepare a note for the windscreen to this effect when some builders in a transit pull in and are confused by the broken ticket machine. I entertain the thought to approach them to advise that 'Chris' from parking control says it's ok – but common sense wins and I just let them dial the number and ask for themselves. Moments later I have locked the car and am on my way.

Walking into town I feel the warmth of the winter sun as it casts softly on the pavement, illuminating the gaps between the tall buildings and softening the chill of a January day. I start to relax into my stride, moving my body in female ways, thinking about how I move my legs, my hips, hold my arms – a subtle dance occurs between the part of me sending out the physical instructions to my limbs, and the part of me that enjoys how my body feels moving this way. I feel connected to my female body in a very real way. I remember early days of exploring my trans self - I tried hip padding and stuffed bras but it always felt false, in-genuine, pretend. Now, by finding clothes that fit, or tailoring the clothes to fit, I feel my real body and inhabit it as female at these times. And although there is many the time when I've entertained ideas of hormones or surgery I come now to reflect on how lucky I am to have a body that works, I'm fit and healthy and to interfere with that starts to feel like vandalism. Yes, over the years I've longed for, yearned for a more feminine shape but I guess I've come to realise the variability of female form, the diversity. The chance of having the ideal body in female form is maybe unrealistic and then I'd end up still being frustrated with my shape but having messed up delicate and complex biochemical systems. Now I find myself in a space where I can redefine what it feels like to have a female body – by simply inhabiting my own as female.

I stride confidently, with a sense of contentment and ease, a pride in myself and my achievement today; and it's not long before I'm passing the Leisure centre where my inner dialogue in distracted by the scene ahead. There is clearly some event taking place, coaches are lined up outside the building and I notice a gaggle of young girls in cheerleader outfits playing and running around outside. Some are having their photo taken. I look enviously at their two colour contrast-pleated skirts – the shape and colour-ways emphasise the movement; the effect. It's a 'very-girl' thing, which is the appeal I guess. As I walk on I contemplate the idea of buying one – maybe eBay, or maybe make one from a pattern – maybe red and white, definitely a couple of rows of piping around the lower hem, I shake the thought from my head and prepare to cross the road and aim for the town centre.

A new realisation hits me with a jolt of anxiety - I have to walk past the bus station, a consequence of the revised parking arrangement. This was not part of the plan: the bus station is a whole new kettle of fish. It's run-down, even for Newport, the people there somehow rougher – the poetic symbolism of derelict people in a derelict building passes through my mind and I wonder if there will be trouble as a couple of drunks walk past heralding perhaps more of what lies ahead. I wrestle with my fears for a moment but can then balance this with an affirmation - today I have an air of nonchalance about me – I am not ashamed to be me, I am entitled to be me, entitled to wear these clothes: today I have pride in being myself and I'm wearing a demeanour that says this. And perhaps as a result it seems I walk through the bus station as if invisible. The paradox of my apparent invisibility amuses me but at least I'm not having to defend myself. I walk up into town and I note that I am not scanning the street for trouble, for once, not hyper-vigilant to threat – no, today I am at ease, striding confidently albeit somewhat femininely towards my first port of call. I enter the department store – the make-up area is in the lobby. I catch the eye of the woman on the make-up counter and we smile at each other and I wave a girly wave to her. The woman on the Estee Lauder counter is there – I recognise her from before. As she serves me I'm not sure she has connected me in grrl-mode with the person there normally in the biker jacket but she serves me with warmth in her eyes and genuineness in her voice. I head to Smiths where I'm after book tabs. Standing at the counter is a young woman with interesting slightly Gothy eye make-up. We smile briefly at each other. I want to commend her on the eye-liner but hesitation gets the better of me – I suspect it's liquid liner she uses. The woman at the till serves me and commends me on the coat – I thank her and quip about bringing a degree of sartorial elegance to Newport.

I head up the main street towards the coffee shop – I've promised myself I will go to Blue Banana – it's only two doors further up. I walk confidently in through the open front door. Here I buy entry purely on the basis of my look. I get a series of appreciative glances from the young staff there. There is admiration and warmth and I enjoy the sense of belonging. A little bit of Camden has found its way onto Newport high street: I scan the displays – there is a gothic-lolita dress in black satin jacquard which is just too adorable, I touch it longingly and regret not having the body to wear it. I wander around seeing what catches my eye as a purchase for today but leave without buying anything, a slight pang of guilt or remorse passes over me - but: a moment later and I find myself in the queue at Coffee #1. The staff smile warmly, I think they recognise me from before but they've not seen me like this. The reception is kind and accepting and I take my order upstairs to a quiet corner. I get my book out and start to read but it's not long before my peace is shattered by the arrival of intruders. A boisterous boy of maybe five, a girl of maybe seven, their Nan and mother. These are not the typical coffee drinkers of Coffee#1 – the Nan remarks to the girl – we'll go to McDonald's later. I think to myself, yeah that's more your scene isn't it, slightly resentful of this Chavvy intrusion into my quiet world – these people are interlopers into my world, a world of refinement, taste, education. They so don't belong here. I am aware of inner hostility towards them, resentment.

The mother of the two children says she'll go downstairs to get the coffee: the Nan asks for a latte.
"A *latter*" questions the woman. (My god, she doesn't even know what a latte is!)
"No *a latte*". Nan's voice is hoarse with a roughened edge but the diction is clear
"*What's a lattay*" The woman shakes her head with a sort of questioning frustration and there's an anxiety underneath the impatience – she is out of her comfort zone.
"*It's a coffee, just get me a latte*". There's impatience in Nan's voice.

I realise the trip to the coffee shop is Nan's idea, maybe this is her type of space. I look at the Nan – there's a warmth about her, something in the lines of her face that tells a story of hardship but underlying humanity, of struggle. Maybe we have a connection beyond appreciation of good coffee. I smile and remark "*that girl needs her palette educated*". She smiles back. Noticing the cheesecake I'm eating she tells me how her mother, one of eleven still likes baking – and despite old age and living in a complex still bakes as if she has eleven to feed. It's touching she's letting me look into her world. I don't know what she makes of me, how she reads me but I feel acceptance from her. The boy is looking up at me – I wink at him and he winks back with a smile. I wonder what messages he has heard about masculinity, about being a boy and what he makes of me. His eye is taken though by a wooden chest set out as a table space. He lifts the lid and Nan and I share a silent concern that he will trap his fingers as he repeatedly slams it shut. She chastises him but it has little effect. Lifting the lid once more he remarks that there is nothing in there. I suggest it's maybe a treasure chest with invisible pirate treasure and a fleeting thought passes through my mind that the coat, earrings and eye make-up could have me passing for Newport's very own Cap'n Jack Sparrow. Actually, Johnny Depp is the same age as me: it's an argument over who wears eyeliner most effectively – ok, damn you Depp and your feminine facial bone structure, I accept defeat! But I digress.

Embarrassed by the boy's disruption to the peace of the coffee shop a frustrated Nan encourages him to go to the window and look for birds. Now I have noticed that despite only being perhaps five this boy has an ear pierced. It's an interesting identifier for masculinity – it seems one ear is manly, two is gay or girly. I have both pierced of course – a legacy of some nifty needlework by my first wife. I remark to him that if he sees any exotic birds he could grab a few feathers and make an earring to go in his pierced ear. (Alluding to the parrot feather earrings I am sporting today).

The little girl has returned upstairs, just ahead of her mother. Reaching in the shopping bags she rummages briefly to retrieve a stuffed toy rabbit. She holds it close to her chest and cuddles it. It's a classic gendered behaviour – the active boy, running around the room, getting into everything, touching everything; and the little girl sitting quietly, cuddling her rabbit and reading the poem on the tag attached to the toy's ear. Reaching in the bag she pulls out a scarf into which she wraps the rabbit, as if to protect it further, keep it safe. The nurturer behaviour to the fore – I can't imagine the boy doing this; being allowed to do this even. The mother sits down and remarks that this is the best coffee she has ever tasted. Now she gets it. I look up at her and we smile at each other in acknowledgement. I continue reading my book.

The book describes the ways boyhood is defined in school with simplistic rigidly applied peer norms – so called hegemonic masculinity, and it reminds me of the exclusion I experienced at school. I broke all the acceptable norms for boy behaviour – boys have to be big strong, into fighting and football, not into being brainy and doing work; boys must be misogynistic and boastful of how they would shag this bird or that. When I looked at the girls I just wanted to be one.

A conversation between mother and Nan starts up as they discuss the boy's hair. The mother wants to buzz cut it - she likes the look of a shaved head on her boy, although Nan seems less keen she does remark that if it gets too long he could look like a girl. A gender rule is communicated – back to opposite sex paradigms, we can communicate our biological reproductive status through hair length.

Two lads in their twenties come up and join the family group and I note anxiety rise within me as I assess the extent to which they might pose a threat. They seem un-phased, and despite occasional interactions with the two women, they mostly talk to each other. Despite my concerns about them they pose me no overt threat and the prejudice it would seem is mine. I continue reading my book for a while and am at ease when a text lands on my phone to say my friend has arrived downstairs. I go to relocate to a larger table and the Nan asks if my move is prompted by the behaviour of the children. Perhaps she had a fear of not-ok-ness, a worry that I was disapproving of them. I reassure her the children are lovely and that I just need a bigger table to meet my friend, she smiles and catching a glimpse of my feather earring remarks

"I see what you mean about getting feathers for an earring".

It's a final moment of mutual validation as we recognise in our own ways that we both feared disapproval, both anxious of the idea of a negative perception by the other.

'To Wong Foo, Thanks For Everything: Julie Newmar' Universal Pictures 1995.

Video Timing: (1:30:08)

Vida (Swayzee) "Oh, Carol Ann, if we really are going to be friends, there really is something I need to tell you ......"

Carole-Ann (Channing) "Adam's Apple: Women don't have Adam's Apples, only men have Adam's apples. And the first night you came to town I noticed you had yourself an Adam's Apple".

Vida (Swayze) "Then you know?"

Carole-Ann (Channing) "I know, but then I'm very fortunate to have a lady friend who just happens to have an Adam's Apple"

Je suis alle aux magasins et ai achete...
(trans: "I went to the shops and I bought...")

Back in school there was a game we played when the French lesson finished early – designed to practise vocabulary and fill the time before the bell went, people would build a shopping list, adding things to the list, and starting with the statement:

"I went to the shops and I bought"

"Mais non, en francais s'il vous plait!" (you'd get told off for speaking in English so this bit is in French – stick with me here!)

"Ah oui, Je suis allé aux magasins et ai achete ..er, ...un chemisier."

"Mais non – un chemise – masculine!" (she's spotted the use of the feminine version of shirt –ie blouse but thinks at this point that my mistake is a symptom of my appalling grasp of her precious subject. I may only ultimately get a D in my O 'level but I know where I'm going with this one!)

Certainement. Je suis allé aux magasins et ai achete er, un chemisier et une jupe. (So, I've repeated my 'mistake' about the shirt and added skirt to the list...I'm playing innocent here but there's a limit)

Mais non!! – vous étes garcon!, vous avez achete le chemise et le pantalons – shirt and trousers, n'est pas (now she's got riled, even she's resorted to using English but I don't correct her. She thinks I'd want to go buy a boy's shirt and trousers. Well duh!!)

"Non mademoiselle, je préfère acheter un chemisier à manches courtes ballon et une belle jupe avec les jolis volants". (translates as: "No, Miss, I prefer to buy a blouse with puff sleeves and a pretty skirt with frills")

Ok I confess, I was anarchic in school, but not entirely reckless – and although it would have been quite funny playing out the above script for real, it had to remain in my imagination for safety, since it would have got me in 360 degrees of trouble – peer group, teacher, school and home and the consequence of that I would not even begin to bear thinking of. But the thought entertains me, and I kinda hope that it's not too long before a transgender person with an anarchic sense of humour can sit in a top set GCSE French class and actually get away with queering a somewhat inane classroom activity just for the entertainment value if not to tell the story of what actually happened 'pendant Les Grandes Vacances'. (This latter exercise was the ubiquitous essay awaiting our return in September, invariably starting with the title, 'During the summer holidays...')

Sadly, I didn't have the nerve to even contemplate buying girl clothes as a teenager, or in fairness the opportunity if truth be told - back then I'd have found myself homeless or dragged to see the psychiatrist if I'd have been caught or worse still confessed to my parents my wish to inhabit girl world some times. It's not easy contemplating ways to experience a world that is denied to you, through some misfortune of biology and at that time I was confused about why I felt different to how I thought I was supposed to feel, and desperately trying to repress any notion of wanting to maybe be a girl.

So I was in my early twenties before I finally plucked up the courage and went to a woman's clothes shop and bought something for myself. In those days I was terrified of exposure – that the person might actually think the purchase was for me – how could I possibly live with the shame? So, I came up with the 'it's for my girlfriend' cover story because obviously if I had a girlfriend then I was NORMAL (ie: heterosexual) and therefore not at all WIERD.   In those early days I would do some reconnaissance, assessing the location and price of the desired purchase and having the money ready so as to make a fast transaction – in and out without being noticed. I bought my first two skirts quite successfully like that.

Christmas would afford the perfect opportunity to buy lingerie since a nervous looking male lingering in the lingerie was par for the course – and of course it's FOR MY GIRLFRIEND! But then, buying a matched set creates a problem - what, 40B bra and size 10 briefs – she's a funny shape for a woman. Preparing a script was an essential element of the planning and reconnaissance stage so being able to go in and say – "I think she's a size 10-12, have you got one like this in that size?" would present what I thought might be read as the performance of uncertain slightly incompetent boyfriend/husband who obviously and reassuringly doesn't really know WAY TOO MUCH about buying girl clothes. I would sometimes add, "I looked at some labels of the stuff SHE wears and it's either 10 or 12 depending" – my cunning subterfuge, a reiteration of the hetero-normative script. Which worked fine until the day I thought I'd treat myself to a leotard. Most women I know hate leotards with a passion mostly it seems because they had to wear them for gym or something and felt very uncomfortable feeling that exposed. I knew I'd missed out on the experience and in the pursuit of finding out and learning about the whole girl experience knew it was a must have. So, one fine day I went to the dancewear shop on the high street of our local town with the imagined specification written on a post-it note as if I'd been sent in on a shopping mission by my beautiful wife. Reading confidently from the note I say:

"Hi – I'm looking for a long sleeve regulation pattern dance leotard in size 14-16 in black or navy"

And this is where my supposedly carefully constructed plan fell to pieces. It turns out they don't come in dress sizes, they have their own classification system so what had started as a confident cover script suddenly disintegrated as I fumbled away and tried to explain it was 'for my wife who just wanted a plain leotard to practice her dance and exercise in'. After a few awkward exchanges I managed to leave the shop now thankfully in possession of said leotard and mercifully it fitted perfectly – I mean, there was no way I would have taken it back if it hadn't! But the experience was really uncomfortable, because I convinced myself they had not believed my cover story and I was back to feeling ashamed. Certainly, after this incident, any confidence I had was blown to pieces and I avoided town shopping for a while.

In those days, shopping on the high street felt very uncomfortable and shame laden and I remember I felt chronically vulnerable to exposure. More often than not I'd see something I wanted but bottle out and leave the store empty handed and frustrated. Many was the occasion when I'd build up to doing a shopping expedition, drive all the way into town, go with the intention of acquiring something, but end up returning empty handed and annoyed with myself for being too afraid to buy it. Mostly I dreaded the idea that the assistant would think I was buying women's clothes for myself whether something was said or not. I think I imagined the assistants gossiping after I'd left and I think I found that idea almost worse. Another anxiety I had was that, with the whole dressing as a girl thing deeply shameful, concealed and secretive, if I took a real girlfriend to the same shop in the future, would the assistant remember me and say something – blowing my cover but this time with my partner – it felt like a significant risk.

After my second divorce in my thirties I had decided to properly engage in exploring my female self and registered for a copy of the Littlewoods catalogue. Catalogue shopping made the whole process a good deal easier since it was entirely anonymous. No embarrassment at the till, just fetch the parcel from which ever neighbour the Postie had left it with and hope to goodness the packaging was still intact. I still feared exposure – as if somehow people would know there was something iffy in me getting clothes from a catalogue. Shame and paranoia make easy and somewhat comfortable bedfellows and I'd wonder what they were thinking as they handed over the parcel to me. It was around this time that the Internet was starting to become more established and this opened up all manner of wondrous possibilities.

The obvious advantage of the Internet is that to the greater extent it is anonymous and as long as the dispatch company assures 'all items sent in plain packaging' it can be a less stressful way of buying clothes and costumes. Nowadays, the Internet has expanded to previously unimaginable proportions and it offers the benefit of support groups, specialist suppliers, and training videos – even illegal hormones! Caveat Emptor on that one girl-friend.

For me to get to a point where I am actually able to go into shops and buy girl stuff though has taken me a long time to get used to and although these days I can do it freely, for a long while I stuck mostly to charity shops, which seemingly afforded a slightly safer place to go. At least you don't have to queue at the till there. I would walk in nonchalantly and whilst heading for the 'legitimate' areas – the men's clothes, the books, the bric-a-brac; my eye would be scanning the women's clothes. And, to their credit, Charity shops mostly afford a cost effective way of experimenting with a wardrobe –working out what works and what doesn't. Paying £2.99 for something that doesn't look good when you get it home is not a problem – chuck it or take it in as a donation. Charity shop purchases can also be hacked about and remanufactured or re-tailored and again if it doesn't work then the loss is not a problem: it's all for charidee!

I've come a long way in developing inner confidence and I find shopping in town a pleasure these days, I can go in dressed in boi-mode or grrl-mode and browse the racks, talk to the staff, pick stuff off the rails, and it feels normal – 'just like a real girl'. I'm aware of how I have shifted from a position of hyper-vigilance to one of being at ease. Over time I have let go of the shame, defeated the thoughts in my head that led to embarrassment and self-consciousness and given myself permission to go and shop. Having let go of the shame I don't need to use the cover story any more, there is nothing to be exposed. Yeah, I want these clothes for me. I just go in, look at what I want, pick what I want; buy what I want. If previously my fantasy was that shop assistants would give me a funny look or make exposing comments then this has turned out to be unfounded. Rather than adopting a posture of shame I can freely walk around the store feeling entitled to buy anything I choose. It's a positive mindset that makes the difference and because I feel good about myself, and happy in the process, I smile at the assistants and they smile back. (Indeed, one even accidentally gave me her phone number the other day but that's another story!)

A major problem for a transgender person finding clothes is the same one most women face it seems. Finding stuff that looks nice and fits well: and having to accept that some things that look adorable, just are not going to work on that frame or with that body. This is the real girl experience. It is useful however to know your dimensions and take a tape measure to check before purchase. I am careful about which items I choose to try on in the shop out of decency – it's a personal choice. I have no qualms however in running a tape measure over the critical dimensions of a garment to check before taking it to the till.

It's an amazing feeling of freedom, walking through a shop and looking at the things you want to be able to buy and knowing that if you have the money you are entitled to buy them – and that doesn't matter if it's underwear, outerwear or make-up. And there will be times when people might be confused but the trick is to leave them with the confusion. If you don't buy into their idea that you are in the wrong then it leaves them recognising that they must be.

The other day I found myself in my local Tesco's, wearing my pink furry boots, cute denim mini-skirt, black tights, blue polo-neck, pink scarf, with my lush new hair and wearing make-up. I'd been to Cardiff in grrl mode, got home and realised there was no coffee. Now applying the safety rule of 'would a young single girl go out in this context' I concluded that my local Tesco was safe enough. So, I'm walking round the store getting stuff like coffee and cat food and a glossy mag. I have self-confidence and am anarchically defiant as I walk round the store, giving people eye contact and smiling at random people. I've learned to inhabit and use my body in more feminine ways, I walk in a more fluid way, how I place my feet, move my hips. I'm enjoying owning my space, reminding myself that I am entitled to be there. And whilst walking round the shop I know I drew a few confused glances but I also knew that they are unfamiliar with transgender people here, AND I knew that aesthetically my outfit worked well. Ultimately, there was nothing threatening in the reactions of others.

And when I reflect on this idea of self consciousness, the idea of feeling vulnerable to comments or unwanted attention I recognised that this is part of the 'real girl' experience too - that attractive women draw glances and comments and mostly from the same type of men that can pose problems for someone like me. I come to accept that part of the reality of being out as transgender is that much of my experience is like that of a natal female. There are some places that a single girl just don't go; there are some places where a woman will draw unwelcome attention and comments from threatening men; being transgender is in that sense just like being a real girl.

A Little Bit Of Lippy (DVD 2006)

(DVD timing 12:05)

Set in Liverpool, Marion Fairley, a young woman in her twenties
arrives at her parent's house in floods of tears...

Mum: He was wearing what?
Marion - A costume.
Mum - An all in one?
Dad - A rubber one?
Marion - Yes
Mum – Oh good Jesus...
Dad - Mary wept!
[Mum is called away to attend Great Aunt Annie on the toilet]
Dad – A woman's, rubber, swimming costume? (he's labouring the
words)
Marion – ..and lipstick.
Dad – fetch my toupee!

Dad leaves to remonstrate with his son in law but its not long before
he returns, further unsettled by events...

(DVD timing 18:45)

Dad – Bloody Drag Queer!
Mum – Queen, Reggie,
Dad - Eh?
Mum - Queen, they call them Drag Queens
Dad – I know what I call 'em. And its unhealthy!
Marion – How do you know
Mum – Yer father were in the territorials Marion, and they were ALL
at it.... all the time.
Dad - In my bloody NAAFI hut!
Great Aunt Annie - it wants reporting..... to the council!

**Originally transmitted by BBC on 16/9/92 and now available on DVD on
Licence to 2Entertain Video Ltd from www.bbcshop.com**

It'll come out in the wash.

The spin cycle complete, Snow White pulled her washing from the trusty old Zanussi, and piled it into the wicker wash basket she always used. And ever mindful to ensure she had properly read the wash instructions for each garment of importance she noted that her favourite dress comprised of a complex formulation of rayon, polyester and acrylic: unlike the remainder of the load, this was clearly not suitable for the modern convenience of a tumble dryer so a short spell on the radiator in the hall would suffice before it was hung back in the dark recess of the closet.

She continued with her domestic chores that morning, busied herself around the house and time passed more quickly than she had anticipated. Now, as I've remarked earlier, the Scot's poet Robert Burns cautions that the best laid plans of mice and men (and in this case Snow White) will 'oft go awry' and remember here dear reader that the intention had of course been for the dress to be safely back in the closet before anyone returned home. That was the intention but, as Snow White had been reminded so many times previously, the road to hell is paved with good intention and so it was perhaps inevitably; ultimately, only a matter of time before all hell would break loose, as it did that day.

"So, er, whose is the snow white dress?" enquired the daughter, with a mixture of incredulity and anxiousness: - albeit mixed with the kind of curiosity that someone of the felis domestica persuasion would invariably be cautioned against. (Of course we might question whether curiosity ever actually was responsible for the premature demise of any cats - I have held to the belief that more often than not it is a lack of curiosity that can be fatal, whether cat or human, but I digress here to distract from a very painful life event). Back to the story as we left it - the daughter has just discovered the Snow White dress on the radiator and is asking to whom it belongs.

Now one might say that there is another useful axiom, which might be invoked at this point, which is, if you don't want to know the answer to the question, you shouldn't ask the question. But the question had been asked.

Ok: so this was not ideal. Indeed, as plans went (and recall that up to this point there had been no plan), this was as far from ideal as you could reasonably get without jetting to the moon on the space shuttle, unpacking the tent and then realising you'd left the front door open back home in 23 Acacia Avenue. There are a handful of moments in your life that change the course of it forever; and sometimes no more than the answer to a single question can be the pivot point: as it was for our family unit. So, it was not by design but miscalculation that I came out to my daughter.

Now, at this particular point in time you might think that surely I could have just lied and yes, that possibility existed: but not for me, not for us. Paradoxically, it was the need to retain and honour the ethic of honesty between us that required the full disclosure. Alternative realities and partial truths could have minimised the significance of the discovery, or provided a cover story, but I loved her too much to insult her, valued our relationship too much to destroy it with deception. Truth hurts, deception really hurts. So I gave her the truth: the whole truth. She was old enough to hear it and understand the complexity – or so I thought. And yet she still ended up very hurt by the process of me coming out to her. I was confused by her reaction and angry with myself for hurting her and yet I thought I had prepared the ground. I thought it would be safe. We had often discussed gender issues and gender politics as it related to her university studies, - even some of her queer friends; we had 'joked' about the pink furry boots under the bed being mine rather than her mum's but somehow this had not prepared her for the disclosure

I think it was hard for her because (as she explained some time later) I represented a constant for her and that constant had suddenly proved itself very different to what she believed. It shook her world and it caused a wound within our family unit that was painful (for all three of us) for a considerable time. Seeing how much it affected her and seeing how hurt she was, re-ignited the internal shame and my female aspects of self went into hiding for quite a while time after that. A few months later, when the initial shock had died down, I showed her me in 'grrl mode'. I stood before her in the pink boots, the denim pleated miniskirt I'd made, a pair of black tights and a plain jumper.

"woah, mum's pink boots"

"No darling, my pink boots"

This time she could comprehend it, integrate it: *"Give us a twirl. Where did you get the skirt?"*

"I made it sweetheart"

"Bloody hell, I didn't know you could sew. Yeah, more bloody things I don't know about you. Hey, maybe you could make me one".

There was an ongoing process of integration and comprehension and thankfully, now I can be more open with her than almost anyone: and if she needs to borrow eyeliner, she borrows mine rather than ask her mum.

The process of coming out to her was an example of just how difficult and painful it can be. And the process of coming out is not a one-off event. There are many occasions, situations and relationships in which you are once again forced to confront the question of whether to 'come out', to reveal the self as different to the assumption made by the other. For many in the queer community a portion of life is lived in stealth, passing as other, passing as the acceptable 'heterosexual matrix norm'. And when I reflect on my many experiences of 'coming out' I note a common theme in my life has been one of testing the water – dropping hints and seeing how they land. Testing the edges of 'just joking' to see how safe it might be: or indeed of discovery and exposure.

My first wife was beautiful and she wore beautiful clothes. She was the kind of girl I'd have liked to have been back then if I had been born 'a real girl'. She was arty, creative; a former punk with hippy leanings and her clothes reflected this. She wore tassled skirts and Indian print tops in the days when this was très chic. I coveted those clothes, especially the tassled skirt which had an elasticated waist and was 'free fit' (ie- would fit me) and another favourite - a long length full flared skirt with a drop basque detail, which shaped the skirt from waist to hip. These were identifiers of girl and not just any girl or woman but of the kind I most identified with. After a year or so of being together I had finally succumbed to the drive to try these forbidden garments on. Ensuring she was out, and going to be out for a while, there was an almost paranoid ritual of marking the position in the wardrobe, the orientation, the folds, so as to place them back precisely, and exactly as before - and thus without discovery. I didn't like the guilt, I didn't like the secrecy but I wasn't sure how she would take the idea of me in a skirt. We were talking one day, I remember sitting with her and the joking and hinting must have pushed over the point of no return when she looked at me puzzled and asked, "what, have you tried my skirt on have you?" I don't like dishonesty in a relationship so 'fessed up – "yeah: a few times, it's nice". She looked a bit shocked but then remarked that if I wanted to wear a skirt then I should buy my own. There was an uneasy tension for sure and whether it was my guilt and shame or her disapproval (or most likely a combination of both) it was very much present, but she had said nonetheless that I should go buy my own: so I think fair enough, and the subject is quickly dropped. Now, one thing that life has taught me repeatedly since then is that people do not always say what they mean, especially in relationships - and so a week and a bit later when I arrived home with my own full flared skirt with the drop basque detail newly acquired from Monsoon there was an uneasiness more than evident when she makes the initial discovery of the carrier bag in the waste bin.

"er, what's the Monsoon bag doing here?"

Ok, I confess - it was a hint – leaving the bag in the bin; I could have just walked in the room wearing the skirt, but I was scared, unsure. I'm wrestling with my own guilt and shame and the possibility of disapproval and rejection so figure the bag in the bin is like a testing the water, sort of soft lead-in. The tension in her voice and her demeanour made the disapproval distinctly tangible. She asked me to put it on and we sat slightly awkwardly that evening to see if we could acclimatise to the notion. I recognise in fairness it was hard for her and although I did wear it a few times more in her presence it just felt unkind to her – she couldn't reconcile the free-living creative hippy pro-feminist beliefs which appreciated a caring soft and tender 'new-age' partner with an underlying subconscious imago that men should be men and therefore just shouldn't wear skirts.

Throughout my second marriage I kept the secret. I had previously painfully learned the lesson that crossing the gender divide was not going to be acceptable and I tried to put the thoughts aside. I had thrown away the small collection of girl clothes I amassed by the end of my first marriage in a symbolic and typical 'wardrobe burning' and decided I would start anew as a 'proper man'. And here, more by accident than design I find my second wife was a different size to me and her clothes wouldn't have fitted even if I wanted to borrow them. And, truth be told, although she was attractive, she didn't wear particularly girly clothes. For the greater part then although I wrestled with the desire to explore female self-expression, I resisted the desire to buy 'girl' clothes: mostly. That said, it was around that time that the Internet really took off and with it a whole new avenue of possibilities for anonymous shopping. Of course, the challenge was to ensure the delivery came when there was no chance of discovery and it was a close thing on a couple of occasions when parcels did not arrive when they were scheduled. Despite a few close calls I did not have to come out to her and my female self was lived in stealth for those years.

After the second divorce I took time to be single. And in that space decided to allow myself to buy and wear female clothes at home. There was a coming out to self in this phase – that given permission to wear nice underwear, skirts, tights I could experience myself in a more feminine way albeit that this was far from easy. Still distinctly shame based I would hide in the house; perform to myself and the mirrored self in an act of vicarious acknowledgement. The person in the mirror sees you and validates your femininity. For a moment you have the enjoyment and excitement of living in the forbidden. Forbidden fruit; forbidden experience. To see yourself as you wish to be seen by others. And also wrestling the other voice, the guilt voice that says you look ridiculous, perverse – that it is wrong and you don't look convincing and you fool no-one.

Over time however, the self acceptance grew and the tensions that previously existed became less. I could now, in the privacy of my own home accept myself in 'girl/grrl mode' and feel less guilt, less shame and actually start to enjoy the process of discovery. I ordered underwear from a catalogue and gradually moved to wearing 'women's' underwear full time. I bought a blue pleated girl games skirt from a charity shop and would wear that. It was a classic marker of 'girl' and I liked it best because it actually hung well. Lets face it here, finding any skirt or dress to hang properly when you have snake hips and no bum is an achievement whatever your chromosomal make-up or nominal gender.

Leading a very busy life and living singly at that time, I had employed a cleaner to come in and assist in managing the household chores. She was amazing – really good at what she did and a genuinely decent person. And it was entirely by accident then that one day I had inadvertently left my blue PE skirt out. Thankfully I was in the house that day and realising that she must have seen it went down to explain. So, suddenly and without preplanning an impromptu coming out process is offered to my cleaner. She was fine with the disclosure and it was never mentioned again. I continue to respect her for that.

With my third marriage I knew that this issue would not go back in the box so before I started the relationship I came out to her– almost as a 'look, don't even bother getting with me, you wouldn't want to if you knew the real me' type way. She did still want to know me and we've been together a long time now. I still don't imagine it is easy for her, particularly in the context of the social stigma that she experiences: and I guess her own confusion over what it all means. And what it means has changed over time. When we first started together I still internalised the shame and kept any feminine aspects of self, hidden from the world. I never imagined at that time going out in 'girl mode'. Over the years though, as I made the journey of discovery, as I increasingly became aware of a drive towards self-actualisation, towards being the true self; that my feminine aspects of self needed to be presented, performed, seen rather than hidden, the desire to be more out increased. Ten years ago I would never have contemplated a time when I would want to go out of the door 'in girl/grrl mode'.

And now my coming out continues. If I go out to the shops in my Ugg boots, black skinny jeans, jewellery, and shoulder bag with toys dangling from the strap am I read perhaps as gay, as trans, as queer? If I wear make-up that forms its own coming out to the people that see me. If I am out in a skirt and boots then these markers of female are juxtaposed against the male frame, the knuckled hands, lack of hips or breasts – and of course the beard which clearly performs transgender, as queer – not woman, not man.

With friends and colleagues the coming out dilemma continues – for some their frames of reference are so constrained it is easier to perform or pass as male to maintain the acquaintance. For others, people closer to me it is so enriching to be self, to present, to perform the female aspects of self in movement, demeanour, expression and clothing.

Coming out is a complex process and one that is endlessly reiterated, re-performed, re-engaged in. Coming out can be hard work. Coming out is liberating.

I feel fine any time she's around me now,
she's around me now,
almost all the time.
And if I'm well you can tell that she's been with
me now,
she's been with me now,
quite a long, long time.
Yes and I feel fine

"From Something In The Way She Moves"
by Singer and Songwriter, James Taylor.

Keep yer hair on!

They say a good haircut can do wonders for a girl's confidence and wow, do I now know what they mean. Today I have a new hairdo and I feel amazing, oozing a new confidence. Sometimes you just know when something is right and looking at the result in the mirror, I just knew it felt right. Today I have beautiful hair, a beautiful layered feather cut, it falls nicely, it feels good, it's a great colour. I'm loving it. I feel a happiness inside that actually feels warm, an internal glow. It's joyous. I don't want to go home - in fact, I want an excuse to go out, to go into town, just be out and about with my new look. Frustratingly, time is against me this afternoon so I have to make it straight back to the car and head for home. But it's a contented journey – albeit I'm careful not to have the window open lest the wind damages the delicate acrylic fibres.

There's an adage – "you pay your money and you make your choice". And this is not the first time I've bought a wig – indeed I've had cheaper wigs before sourced over the Internet and costing around £50 and they were ok, adequate. But they never felt quite right, very much felt like wearing a wig. And the fit on these was loose so I was ever anxious about them moving or coming off; having to be endlessly careful about how to move the strands out of my face, and it's not like you can just flick the fringe sideways as you do with natural hair. A wig had always been a poor compromise to the loss of real hair. I miss having my long hair.

In my early twenties I had finally reached a point where I could let my hair grow long. Now self-employed, I was freed of the discrimination of employers that let women have long hair but not me. It was nonetheless a phase in my life where I remember struggling with the issue of gendering my identity – caught between an idealisation and aspiration toward the feminine but a strong need to present as masculine – as a proper 'man'. It was very binary, and my outward appearance to others was being performed as male and was being further masculinised by my job as a builder and by its associated visual rubrics – dirty torn jeans, dusty shirt, rugged work boots. I could show the world I was a real man because I did manual work, proper men's work. I looked like a MAN. And this despite having shoulder length hair which in the 1980's was less common on men than the previous decade. A cunning ruse but it seemed to fool 'em!

Having long hair while doing manual work, especially in dirty environments has its down side and tying it back could minimise the damage, make it more practical. I remember the first time I tied my hair back in a ponytail. I was very unsure about this but was being encouraged by my wife of the time. She didn't at that point know about the battle going on inside me about how to identify my gendered self, she read me as male, she thought of me as male. She saw tying your hair back in a ponytail as ok for a male- it was a practical solution. I was excited and anxious – it felt girly to have a ponytail but that was inside my head, and outwardly I was trying to convince the world I was male, a proper man.

Having accepted that tying long hair back was ok for a man, one still had to observe the rule that a low-neck ponytail is masculine, a high ponytail feminine. It would be another twenty or thirty years before the likes of David Beckham could emerge with a top strand ponytail or a snooker player appear in public wearing a headband.

In my thirties, following my divorce I had relocated to Wales and decided to go into teaching rather than start a new building business. I'd loved building but the work was killing me and I'd seen people left crippled with arthritis after a working life on the tools. So, I went to Uni and did a teaching degree (doing bits of building work in the holidays to pay for it though – the old adage, learn a trade and you'll have something to fall back on ever true!). At Uni one of the girls had her hair tied back with something called a 'Scrunchie'. Up to this point, hair ties were thin elasticated bands or a towelling type, relatively minimal. The Scrunchie was a new fashion, more blatant, yet softer, more girly and I loved it. I wanted one but wrestled with whether I'd get away with it. How far could I push the boundary without giving the game away – I didn't want people thinking I was not a proper 'man' but I coveted the satin blue Scrunchie that Sarah wore. In the second year I bought one and seemed to get away with wearing it – nobody commented. Even sometimes wore my ponytail to the side with the Scrunchie just on my shoulder – nobody commented.

As the course drew to its natural conclusion, the reality of having to get a job in a school hit home. And I was terrified: not about having to stand in front of thirty or more hardened and disaffected youth in some dive state comp, no I was looking forward to that. I was terrified that I'd have to get my hair cut to get a job. Throughout the course nothing was said, but then, in the final term of the final year the course tutor dropped a snide comment one day as she passed me in the corridor: this just compounded my fears. Finally, interviews for placements were being held and I met the deputy head of a school in Cardiff where I would teach for a term. The interview went well and she seemed to like me. At no point had the obvious fact of my long hair come up in the discussion and as the interview went on and time progressed I was increasingly aware of a sinking feeling. I awaited an uncomfortable inevitability – and as my stomach churned and the tension and hollow feeling in my throat that accompanies nausea built, I felt like a condemned man: I had to say something, so taking a deep breath, my heart pounding, my head buzzing, I swallowed briefly to encourage my stomach contents back down to where they belonged and said:

"I guess you've noticed I have long hair, I hope that's not a problem"

My heart was in my mouth, and thoughts raced through my head, trying to prepare myself and rationalise what she was about to say.

"No that's fine, that's not a problem. Obviously just keep it tied back neatly at work".

I can't find words to explain the elation and sense of relief because it was so extraordinary: at that point I knew then that I could be ok, that this established a precedent and that if she could be cool with this then so could others. I'd been spared the execution. And got myself a placement into the bargain. I had a job in teaching. That was a good day.

It's funny how things work out in life: having chosen to go into teaching I'd sort of imagined myself working in some rough comprehensive school inspiring the disaffected yoof of a troubled housing estate to believe in themselves and I could be there, somehow bringing out potential that others had missed. And yet, as I emerged from Uni with my new teaching degree I entered the job market at a time when my subject had just been erased from the core curriculum and there were now no jobs. Especially in the state sector. And by bizarre twist of fate I find myself teaching in a private girls school, a job which I did for about a dozen years and loved every moment. Working in private education was not how I'd imagined it would be, and neither was single sex education. I learned a lot from the experience there, overcame my internal bias and preconceived notions, and was ultimately reminded of the truism that prejudice is born of ignorance. My prejudice towards private education had been borne of the childhood messages passed on by others and adopted, from both home and playground. The reality was very different, certainly in my case.

Being a male teacher in a girl's school but having long hair confused some; especially the younger year groups. I remember an open day when prospective parents would bring their darling offspring to view the facilities. A women in smart clothes and of very tidy appearance was hauling a similarly presented small child along a corridor when the child caught sight of me. With wonderful childish naivety and a youthful voice that carried beautifully along the hollow echo of the long corridor she asks,

"Why's that man got girl's hair?"

I smiled to myself and imagined for a moment turning to her and explaining that it's part of my pro-feminist political statementism; a deconstructivist approach to challenge gender binaries, to help the girls challenge their internalised gender constraints. I decide instead to carry on walking and chuckle to myself with a degree of schadenfreude at the mother's embarrassment. Kinda mean huh?

Back in my teaching room I had a poster. A poster of a woman in a beautiful velvet fitted dress wearing a piece of contemporary neck jewellery. I'd spotted the picture at an exhibition in Birmingham of contemporary jewellery and art and chose it because was such a stunning image. This young woman, shaven headed, holding a thick metal bar suspended on a ring around her neck in a deliberately aggressive pose, and wearing this beautiful velvet dress. I captioned the picture – "Jewellery: something you wear to make yourself look pretty" which was of course a partial and double irony, beauty being in the eye of the beholder, prettiness rather subjective. Oftentimes, especially at the start of a new academic year, a host of first year pupils would come into the room and be confused by the image. A male teacher with a ponytail; and a poster of someone with very short hair wearing a beautiful velvet fitted dress.

"Is that picture a man or a woman?" they would invariably ask. And this is intriguing from the perspective of what is being read as male and female. The girl in the picture filled the dress perfectly, her figure undeniably woman. And yet her crew cut suggested to these young girls that this person must be male. What do you read – boobs or hair. At age 11 it seems hair length is the easiest demarker.

As I reached my late thirties my hair had been getting thinner and thinner, and gradually scalp was becoming more and more visible. Each time I washed it the thinness seemed more noticeable until eventually I knew the situation was no longer tenable and one dreadful summer holiday I had to succumb to the indignity of the hair clippers. There was no point in having hair if I couldn't have it long so I cut it all off. It took time to adjust but I'd been preparing for that moment and knew I had to accept it. And since that time, I've had to live a life presenting a no.2 crew cut to the world, my identity betrayed by a genetic and hormonal time-bomb that robbed me of my lovely long hair. Even now, years on, seeing myself in the mirror never quite feels right – it doesn't look like me as I want to be; and I've missed the feel of having long hair.

Obviously, since losing my hair there have been many occasions where I have mourned the loss: and yet, the other day on a conference in Cardiff I had a spooky vision of myself from a parallel universe. A transsexual woman: similar facial features as me, similar figure and her own hair – as mine had become, long but spindly thin, frayed and frazzled at the ends. She needed a decent haircut truth be told and here is the paradox, the idea of long hair as female identifier is for her the identifier that gives the transgender status away in this case. If I'd had GRS surgery I think I'd have probably ended up looking like that. If she wanted to be read as a real woman then the paradox was that shorter hair would have made it look better, more convincing. So it's ironic that the 'feminine' long hair gave the game away – it just didn't look right, not for a born-biologically-female-woman.

In this journey then of self-realisation, of developing and achieving a congruent transgender self I have reflected on what it is that creates an aesthetically authentic look. And there are times when I miss having long hair, and given that buying wigs off eBay may be convenient and broadly speaking satisfactory I knew that better was possible and to that end I figured it was time to have a proper wig, properly fitted and styled: and this would mean a trip to a wig specialist.

I remember once, a couple of years back in fact, meeting a self-identified transvestite called Joanna at a gender workshop who was telling a group of mostly women how much a new wig had cost – Joanna thought that £150 for a hairdo was a lot of money. I don't think they agreed, I guess by comparison to being 'a real girl' that kind of money once a year was great value – I mean a cut and colour at Toni & Guy will set you back that kind of cash every six weeks. So the women weren't particularly impressed. Sadly, we didn't get to see the wig as Joanna is only out on rare and carefully planned outings and on this occasion Joanna was having to do 'boy-mode'.

So, finding a wig specialist had me reaching fer good ol' yeller-pages and looking through the listings. As I flicked through the pages, a slight feeling of apprehension and uneasiness was being tempered by the internal reassurance that this was an ok thing to do and I started to balance the anxiety with a degree of optimism and hope. An advert caught my eye – she was based in Cardiff, private consulting rooms, and she specialised in hair pieces and wigs for people with medical conditions such as cancer and alopecia as well as cosmetic applications. An intuitive part of me picked up a good vibe from this advert and I quickly jotted down her number. Now, one thing I am learning in this journey is that being a grrl is all about attitude – so without shame I called her.

"Hi, I found your advert in yellow pages, I'm transgender and looking for a good quality wig, I've tried cheap ones off the Internet but would like a properly fitted one"

She was fine with that, so we booked our first consultation.

A week later, the big day has arrived and I've driven into Cardiff for a 9 o'clock appointment and discovered that I have significantly underestimated the impact of rush hour traffic. Now I hate being late and I thought that an hour to do a journey of 12 miles should have left plenty of margin. Today I am wrong and I arrive late, embarrassed by the lateness (but importantly I note to myself, not the whole being queer thing): I am nonetheless, greeted at the door of this Victorian former town house by a woman with a warm smile. For this first visit, I'm playing it low key: my skinny black jeans, my Uggs, bit of jewellery, and a sparkly blue scarf to complete the ensemble. We go up the stairs to her salon: the room seems quite large, the ceiling is tall and there's a huge bay window looking down on the traffic below: on the wall opposite the door my eye is taken by a series of shelves, with row upon row of polystyrene heads in wigs. It's a slightly unnerving moment, slightly surreal but it's ok, I am here to buy a wig and this is what a wig shop looks like. I've not done this before and I'm nervous, but she seems friendly, accepting and I am reassured by the obvious privacy she affords her customers – whatever their need or motivation.

She helps me feel at ease as we exchange small talk about the heavy traffic and then settle down to business. I show her the two wigs I currently use and explain the problem. I have a small head – most the time this is not strictly speaking a problem except when maybe buying a baseball cap as I end up having to buy ladies or child size. At 5'8" tall it's not that I'm especially small, just I seemingly have a small head. This is also a problem when it comes to buying wigs as I have already discovered and the result of this reality means that the basic range (about the £150 region) are now ruled out and I'm having to select from the middle shelf – the 'petite' range. We try one from this shelf – the cut is not me but the fit is excellent. It feels snug, secure: perfect. Now, the look I'm going for is something akin to how my hair was before male pattern baldness killed the roots and left it too thin to have in anything other than a crew cut. We try a couple of others, mostly to assess the colour rather than the cut.

"You want the 'myu'" she says, pointing to a slightly forlorn looking bald polystyrene head sitting at the end of the row. "It's out of stock but I can get one in for you"

She sets about describing it and it sounds devine: a layered feather cut, longish swept fringe, 'really lush' apparently. She's talking my language. It's £280 quid. Yikes.

In my head I've set aside a budget – this is double that - and I'm rushing now to rationalise it in my mind. We discuss the need to look after the wig properly and we are adding a polystyrene head and anti-static spray. The total comes to just over £300. I'm trying to look nonchalant despite the battle going on inside me about how much this is all going to cost. I remind myself that we seldom regret our extravagant purchases, only our economy ones, so – hey, it's only money and I've tried cheap and cheap ain't no good. Cheap just ain't lovely. So, having processed this thought train in the time it's taken her to get on the phone to the supplier to check on stock levels I've bitten the bullet and we are booking an appointment for the following week.

The intervening week passed quickly and I'd scheduled a day in Cardiff in grrl-mode, meeting up with a colleague to discuss some ideas for promoting and supporting LGBT issues more generally before heading across town to the salon. This time I arrive just on time for my appointment. I'm feeling upbeat, a bit excited, a bit nervous. I've enjoyed the feeling of being out and about doing grrl-mode and today it's going well. Today, I'm out and wearing a really cute little black skirt over black leggings combo. The skirt is gorgeous, mid thigh length mini, flared and in a soft cotton mix that gives it really nice movement. I'm wearing my Uggs today, the proper ones. And I've done a bit of eye make-up – not too much though and I'm pleased with the effect: subtle but distinctly noticeable.

We pull the first wig out if its box and try it on. The fit is excellent and the look is good. But is it perfect; is it worth £300 quid. The other one is a slightly different colour. We try this one on and bingo, this is it - colour is perfect, fit is perfect. It's a done deal. Ten minutes later I'm leaving her salon with a large bag under my arm and now wearing my new hair.

I get home and it's not long before I have to get ready for work so the hair goes on the polystyrene stand on the dressing table and I return to being shaven headed. I take off my make-up but decide to put a light touch back. Now I've got better at applying make-up with a lighter touch I'm sometimes wearing a bit while working. Nobody has commented.

The wig sits on its stand for a few days before another opportunity presents itself. With a day at home to do stuff I decide to do the whole hair, make-up, skirt thing and enjoy some girl time. We get a phone call from the darling daughter who wants to come over. I still struggle to know how well she copes with the transgender thing and I contemplate changing. I decide against, she'll be on her own so I text her to drop a hint that my hair is 'longer than last time she saw me'. She texts back about a weird dream she had about me in a wig. She's got the hint. An hour later her she arrives and slightly anxiously I greet her at the door.

"My god, he really looks like a woman – minus the beard of course. Less scary than I thought."

It's the first time she's seen me wear make-up, even though she knows I do, and it's the first time she's seen me in a wig. I think it's a lot to take in but she manages stoically. Her reaction says something about the impact of hair as a visual code for gendered identity. Her reaction says she still accepts me. I still get my hug.

The celebration of a transgender identity is always I guess tempered by the knowledge of the impact on others. I want to celebrate my new hair, wear it all the time but I'm not alone on this journey, and whilst it's becoming easier for me to accept myself, it's taking time for important people around me to come to terms with what it all means.

Richard O'Brien's
"The Rocky Horror Picture Show"
(1975)

Don't get strung out
by the way that I look.

Don't judge a book by its cover
I'm not much of a man
By the light of day
But by night I'm one hell of a lover.

I'm just a sweet Transvestite
From Transsexual Transylvania.

Featuring Tim Curry as 'Frankenfurter'.

Gay dear, me dear, no dear!

So, I'm stood in this bar in Newport, South Wales wearing a pair of black thigh high, stiletto heeled leather boots, black lace tights over a pair of grey opaque tights which created a rather good look if I do say so myself; an adorable red brocade miniskirt complete with tulle underskirt; a heap of silver jewellery, full on smoky-eye make-up, my top hat and a vintage frock coat, and I've never felt safer in a bar or pub in my life. Now there is a context to this you'll appreciate, but I wanted to make the point that we need to challenge our assumptions. The event is a Burlesque evening and it's being held in a gay bar in the back end of Newport which surprised me – firstly that Newport could cope with a gay nightclub and that Newport could actually find people to appreciate the subtlety of a burlesque evening and not expect something seedier. It turns out I am wrong on both counts and it's a really enjoyable evening; good-natured and with a really friendly crowd. Now, the notion of being seen in a gay bar or knowingly going to a gay night club is not something I would ever have previously contemplated, again my own prejudice here, born out of the social conditioning of school and home and without evidence of experience. And yet the experience of that evening was really positive and in all honesty, not actually the first time I've been in a gay bar or club.

The first time I went to a gay bar had been on an occasion a few months previously where I found myself stood in a place called 'Bar Code', a gay night club in Soho, wearing my cute denim miniskirt, grey opaque tights, black thigh high stiletto heeled boots, eye make-up and silver jewellery. Here again, I felt incredibly safe – people were respectful, peaceful. People were there to enjoy a good night and it felt very different to any club or pub I'd previously been in. The bouncer on the door of the club in Soho also challenged my assumptions and internal prejudice. In fairness and credit to him, he was brilliant – there we have this great big 'brute' of a man – the kind who as a kid, I would have seen as being a problem for me, particularly at school - but here he was, asking to check our bags before we went in and yet entirely charming and respectful. He made me feel welcome to his club and his attitude left me with a real sense of entitlement. And similarly back in Newport at the burlesque evening, the bouncers waved me through politely and the only 'trouble' all night was from a rather sweet but slightly tipsy lesbian who took a shine to my top hat and wanted to borrow it to have her picture taken. She took it and disappeared for a while and yet, true to her word she brought it back about a quarter of an hour later, in perfect condition. Now you might wonder where this is leading....

Probably one of the most depressing books I have read in the journey of self-discovery, and in the researching of this book is Martino & Pallota-Chiarolli (2003) "So What's a Boy?" That book, a recent research project conducted in Australian secondary schools was a painful reminder to me of the way homophobia and misogyny drove so much of the bullying and intimidation which was a key part of my childhood experience back in the 1970's, and still continues to be prevalent within Western schools culture today. Here we are in the 21st century, and yes there has been progress since back then but we have a long way to go. I'd spent some time this week reading up on the latest Welsh Assembly guidance for schools on anti-discriminatory policy and marvelled at the idealised notions set out in the documentation. It's great stuff in theory but will we see it implemented in practice? I can't say the ideas promoted in these policy documents in any way resembled my own experience of being in schools, either as a pupil back in the 1960's and 1970's or indeed as an adult working within schools in the 1990's.   When I taught PSE (Personal, social and health education) I made a point to try to include LGBT elements, to get the pupils to question the gender and relationship norms they had been previously taught. With a group of year 9 girls I once set them the challenge of deciding how they would raise a son or daughter differently, what would be the important things to tell them about the difference.   This threw up some interesting anomalies – pupils who recognised feminist and equality ideals but also fought powerful internal imagoes – it confused them to think that somehow they saw art as a girl subject, electronics as boy, the idea that certain subjects were more suited to boys than girls but they weren't sure where they had got that idea from, that even musical instruments could be divided along gendered lines – girls play flute, boys play guitar, girls play cello, boys play drums. It made them think.

Subtly but powerfully ingrained within the culture are these gender and sexual delineators, internalised without question. An exercise like the one described above facilitated a process of questioning – we asked who had taught them these things, who had led them to believe it. Some just thought it had always been, that they'd just always thought that, no one had taught them. In the absence of question, assumption becomes reality. And the assumption of heterosexuality and hetero-sexist gendered identities as 'normal' and thereby privileged by virtue of its status as a supposed dominant default, leaves 'other' identities as lesser (and here we might acknowledge that white and able-bodied would be seen as additional codicils).

Note above that I use the word 'other' in quotes here quite deliberately to denote the ubiquitous and subtle process of oppression that arises through a process called hetero-normativity. For a young person growing up with a queer identity, be that Lesbian, Gay, Bisexual or Transgender, if the assumption within school is that there is only one type of gendered identity to have, one type of sexuality to have and the people in authority are seemingly colluding in this message, then identities that are 'other' become subordinately positioned, in ways that we might also observe in relation to ethnicity and disability.

A recent Stonewall survey (Hunt & Jensen 2007) showed that even now, teachers generally fail to respond to or challenge the use of homophobic language or take appropriate action to challenge homophobic bullying. But getting teachers and other adults to recognise the impact of homo-phobic put downs and understand the need to start to challenge this in the way that racism is being, will take time. I still found girls would be called 'lezzers' (think of changing the z for s and see what it does to the word); boys would be called gay or 'bender' as a way of 'othering', a put down: as something undesirable. In fact, designed to be pretty much still the ultimate put down truth be told. As I became more aware of the significance then of homo-oppressive language - of the ways in which words and phrases created subtle but significant ways to disadvantage people I started to challenge it. And yet challenging the use of these phrases was typically greeted with a kind of "that's what's wrong with this country, political correctness gone mad, there's nothing wrong with calling someone gay – we don't mean anything by it". Well, if it wasn't a put down ya wouldn't use it duh! Here we see the creating of 'other' and 'other as lesser' through a subordinating discourse that positions the dominant in-group as more powerful and in the case of the male-homophobic injunction, I would assert not so much the sexual desiring of same sex body but a perception of effeminacy and thereby linked to the denigration of the feminine through culturally accepted misogyny.

To achieve the noble ideals of the proposed legislation will necessarily involve a lot of education of the educationalists – helping them overcome their own homophobia – and it's not that I excluded myself in that thought, although I believed I was unprejudiced, I came to learn how subtle the internalisation of homophobia is, and that unwittingly, legacy thoughts still contaminated my approach. Disappointingly, when I taught at secondary level there were still teachers more openly overt in their disapproval of same sex relationships, who could not validate a gay identity and who would refuse to teach some of the PSE program because it mentioned homosexuality. Sadly, some saw nothing wrong joining in with homophobic discrimination and naming.

As an amusing aside here, I remember covering a Year 10 English lesson one day, and in a discussion with the pupils pointed out that the Shakespearean Sonnets they had studied were not necessarily hetero-sexual, but actually quite probably homo-erotic according to current thinking. Some academics certainly believe that they were written to a young guy called William Herbert, third earl of Pembroke who was a patron of the bard. It puts the sonnets and the writing in a much more interesting light if true and offers insight into the idea of repressed sexuality, and of the context of living a false life through cultural oppression. Intelligent year 10 pupils can cope with that level of insight and reflection and yet when the English teacher returned from her absence she was, shall we say, 'more than displeased' that I had put this idea to them which left me thinking that perhaps she knew a good deal less about Shakespeare than she might like to profess. Many famous artists, musicians and historical figures have had LGBT identities but this is invariably glossed over in schools leaving these identities invisible and we therefore as a society are missing a valuable opportunity to normalise 'other' ways of being

In the absence of this process of validating other identities we are left with a depressing reality, a picture still being painted of continuing chronic intolerance to diversity within schools (whether race, disability or gendered identity) that sets out strict hierarchies and dichotomous structures. These structures are formed and policed by the young people themselves in what Martino & Pallota-Chiarolli refer to as panopticonic policing. It's an interesting phrase.

In 1785, social theorist Jeremy Bentham proposed a new design of prison with the intention of controlling prisoners in psychological rather than physical ways. Known as the Panopticon it was a radical design which relied on the notion that prisoners could be observed at all times, often without knowledge of where they were being observed from in what Bentham described as a 'sentiment of an invisible omniscience'. Prisoners could not break the rules because they knew they were probably being observed, they just couldn't be sure. The design was proposed as a way of reducing the staffing costs since if one didn't know where the guards were, one couldn't know how many were there – hence one needed less guards. It's this sense of invisible policing forces, guards observing one's behaviours from any number of unknown vantage points, and ready at a moments notice to punish transgressions, that sums up nicely for me the idea of panopticonic policing in relation to gender and sexual identities, that is a part of school culture predominantly, and broader culture to the lesser extent.

So, I found school hard, not fitting in, feeling excluded by this policing of acceptable gendered behaviour, executed and governed mostly by my peer group, although oftentimes with the collusion of adults within my social system. And the thing that mostly identified me as 'other' was a perception of effeminacy, that I was not manly enough, that I was a bit too girly for my own good and therefore, the logical conclusion was that I was gay which left me desperate to not be. I learned that to be 'boy' is to be 'NOT girl' and therefore I learned the need to endlessly endeavour to hide any feminine aspects of self, to dissociate from any idea of being thought of as gay. So whilst it was ok that other people were gay – I could have some sympathy with their plight, I just didn't want to get lumped into that group since it carried so much implicit disadvantage and potential for exclusion and potential harm. For a long time though I was not fully aware of how powerful this negative injunction was. One day I had a light bulb moment.

I was up in London at a conference on lesbian and gay issues – this was a few years ago and at a time when my female identified self was limited to exploration within the confines and privacy of my own home and I only performed a male gendered self to the world outside. The presenter was exploring the idea of internalised homophobia. I sat there, smugly thinking, "I don't have homophobia, I'm not prejudiced, I'm cool with gay people" and then he challenged us with this question:

"Would you be seen sitting in a café or travelling on a bus reading a copy of Gay Times?"

And my automatic answer? "No, someone might think I'm gay". Immediately, an uncomfortable truth dawned on me and this was of course the point of the exercise. Even as an adult, I didn't like the idea of someone thinking I might be gay. So, what exactly is wrong with the idea of someone thinking you are gay we might ask. A penny dropped, the programming, the socialisation was so powerful, so pernicious that elements remained and it infected and contaminated my psyche in ways that I had not fully appreciated.

It's complicated then, particularly when gendered identity and sexuality have been confused in the naive and misogynistic injunctions of the school playground. A part of you wants to self identify as female and embrace and embody elements of the feminine. And yet to adopt anything identified as feminine is to be effeminate and therefore GAY and of course being thought of as gay is a bad thing because being gay apparently is bad. It's an ongoing battle to recognise and challenge the negative automatic thought that enters the mind on these occasions and balance it with a more adult, more realistic appraisal. I smiled this morning as I caught those thoughts flash through my mind as I reached to use the anti-wrinkle cream and moisturiser on my face and set about tinting my eyelashes with some 45 day mascara. In the journey to embrace and work more creatively, and more openly with a transgender identity I have had to challenge my own internalised homophobia, my own injunctions against homosexuality, my own negative associations. I hate the internal voice that looks at a male dancer on a cookery program and says – 'he's a bit poofy' because the voice is there before I can challenge it. I have to hear it, recognise it, be annoyed with myself for thinking it and then let go of the need to be threatened by his apparent effeminacy. I don't know how long it takes to get rid of those thoughts: in the mean time I just have to recognise and challenge them. And this explains why using moisturiser was not something I could do previously – it's a girl thing and that would make it a gay thing. Men have rough skin – be a proper MAN. I recognised that I had created a split between the part of me that was trying to be a proper male and the part that wanted to be feminine. I had my own internal binary, my own dichotomous gender structures, and that led me to reflect on the extent to which this phenomenon exists for others who cross the gendered lines.

I am aware that for some males who cross-dress it seems to give permission to have a sexual relationship with a man that would not be permissible within their male identified selves. As if the idea of being gay is so bad that it's easier to dissociate that aspect of self to an alter-ego. I think I get their struggle albeit having a sex change is a rather dramatic solution to a societal problem of intolerance of diversity unless of course you live in a place like Iran where it becomes essential. (see Drescher 2010).

For my part, I recognise that I have a lot to thank the Gay Pride movement for. Childhood had been uncomfortable - endlessly called a poof; queer; sissy or just gay but in a society that is becoming more accepting of a gay identity it becomes easier to be out as gender-queer. In this personal journey that sought to create a way of 'doing' transgender, I reached a point where I didn't feel the need to 'pass' or present as a 'real girl', a 'woman', the idealised 'heterosexual natal female' [the supposed acceptable identity second only in rank desirability to heterosexual male] – nope, I can be out as transgender, doing gender-blending and whether that makes me lesbian or not I guess is open to interpretation. I'd say it's academic.

Reiterating this point then, I'm asserting that to some degree, to hide in the closet is to be a fugitive of the system – hiding from the apparent authority of the socio-political system of gendered identity and policed sexual identities. To present as other, or endeavour to 'pass' is to maintain and implicitly thereby reinforce the system. But, what if I could 'pass'? I contemplate the thought again.

Would I pretend I was 'all woman' under the acrylic wig, the stubble concealing foundation, the foam padding and the silicone bra fillers, affected falsetto voice; - would that be easier? I recognise that when I was younger I could have got away with it; now in later life I realise that I fool no one in pretending. And more importantly it feels in-genuine to me too and that has been an important realisation.

Would I have surgery? Lord knows many times I have contemplated it – as if corrective surgery would cure my apparent defectiveness and make me a 'real woman' and thus fit more neatly into the heterosexual matrix of male female; man with woman; woman with man. I defy the matrix and I'm not alone: Kate Bornstein is interesting in this regard having started as natal male, had gender reassignment surgery to become 'female' but now identifies as transgender. I admire that.

As I draw this chapter to a close I hope to have illustrated that a significant block to me exploring and embracing my transgender identity over the past four decades has been inextricably linked to the internalised homophobia of childhood. A powerful and almost unconscious element of the inner turmoil and emotional struggle was caught up in this historical fear of homosexuality, the fear of being thought of as gay, and of reiterating those taunts back at myself when ever I did things that echoed or identified with femininity. Especially in the early days when I might momentarily allow myself a foray into girl-world and then recoil in horror at what it meant for me to be doing that – the punitive inner voice recreating the internalised panopticonic presence of an oppressive and disapproving society. To transcend the oppression, to reject the defectiveness and to be able to walk down the street unashamed is where freedom begins. In any case, to be a 'real girl' is an abstract idea. Who knows what it feels like to be male; to be female? We can only know the extent to which we fit our culturally expected norms – in which case I ain't neither, I am both. I am transgender.

It's a .....

My friend Alex has a shop, and it's a lovely shop. It's full of really pretty stuff – beautiful home furnishings, exquisite jewellery, heavenly hand made soap with rose buds adorning the surface, divine bath bombs that fizz in the water and scent your bath with exotic herbs like ylang-ylang or jasmine. As you enter the shop a heady perfume pervades, soft music plays, this is a multi-sensorial experience. Standing in the middle of this small shop you find display stands with hand made greetings cards with clever little sayings and quirky postcards and fridge magnets with girlie in-jokes and feminist mantras. Shelves stacked with little objects and curios, decorative trinkets. This is a girlie shop and no mistaking, an oestrogen rich emporium that embraces you in a cuddly blanket of the feminine and lays out before you an enchanting array of girl-stuff - and that doesn't take a masters degree in gender studies to work out – it's kinda obvious to anyone who entered. And to its credit, for the hapless male, shopping for an ideal girlfriend-gift it offers a reassuring certainty that almost anything in there would be the perfect choice. She stocks some very tasteful things it has to be said!

And back last spring, walking into town one bright and sunny morning, I found the shop front adorned with a huge banner and display proclaiming:

"IT'S A GIRL"

The banner, indeed the whole shop front announced not just the arrival of her new baby which was a joyous thing, but the thing that would be most important for people to know: –the all important, "What is it? – oh, IT'S A GIRL". To make the point, the window was awash in pink. Everything in the display was a shade of pink. That is because PINK IS A GIRL COLOUR. If you are a girl you wear pink, you like pink and everything you play with has to be pink, or lilac, or maybe purple but generally only to contrast with the PINK. I've been to Toys 'R' Us, I know this stuff.

And for my part, I love pink. But I think I love pink mostly because it signifies girl – if I wear pink it lets me tell the world that I AM A GIRL TOO.

And yet historically the whole 'girls like pink thing' is relatively new. Victorians didn't dress boys in blue and girls in pink – for them boys and girls were dressed in white dresses for the first few years of childhood, and then beyond that, colour was not seemingly delineated. It's only after the Second World War that we see the much stricter delineation of gender colour and the setting of blue as the boy colour. Arguments abound as to the rational for this but there may some validity in the assertion that the choice may have been influenced by the tradition of making formal military uniforms in blue. The blue-coat tradition started in Tudor times with blue being the cheapest dye available then, so it was used for the uniforms of boys attending some of the new charitable schools. There are various literary references from before the 1950's however that specifically state pink as an appropriate colour for boys since it was in the same family as red – seen as a dramatic colour. Blue, being calmer, was seen as more appropriate historically for girls and blue is of course the colour we see worn by the Virgin Mary in much catholic iconography. After the Second World War however, and possibly fuelled by the emerging affluence of the middle class was the opportunity to dress children in brand new clothes as a signifier of wealth and here a fashion develops to perform and denote hierarchy, status and identity in the choice of the child's clothes – at this point pink is for girls, blue for boys. Another arbitrary and constraining binary had become thus established.

And so we might reflect then on the ways in which, from the moment of birth or in some cases before a baby is even born, (for those that have taken the opportunity to find out in advance the apparent reproductive status of their child) there is an implicit and explicit process of setting out a predetermined and authorised modality of being boy-or-girl. So even for the feminist friends of mine who endeavoured to deconstruct gender rules for their children, was an awareness that although biology has instilled certain traits (albeit these were not exclusive to either sex but subject to nature's randomness to some extent) there was a much greater influence to be overcome in the form of a cultural milieu and societal meta-indoctrination which acted in so many domains from outside – the peer group, children's books, television, toys, and even the school system.

Of course, there are the parents who had never joined the feminism bus, who do not embrace equality and gender fluidity, but recreate in their family micro-culture the historic patriarchy that existed even prior to the 1950's; residual pockets of resistance within society that reinforce gender disadvantage and misogynistic oppression, and pass it on to the next generation as their norm: to each their own.

And then there are the parents who struggle to cope with their own fragile ego when it's their child who does not meet the predetermined gender role expectations. And herein lies the potential for real tragedy.

I met a woman who had a problem. Her husband was apparently "YOUR TYPICAL MAN'S MAN". Big and tough and liked his sports and liked his beer even better. He was THE MAN OF THE HOUSE even in her own words. But she loved him; he was her BIG STRONG MAN – every girl's dream guy apparently. And when she gave birth to their first child he was over the moon – IT'S A BOY! Within hours of this young person entering the world, the remains of umbilical cord still dangling from the pale pink tummy of this beautiful baby, his father had hot-footed it into town to place a significantly large bet with the book-maker that asserted:

"THIS BOY WILL PLAY RUGBY FOR WALES".

Now, chuckle you might since this will not have been the first time a guy, overjoyed at the wonder of childbirth and the delight of being a new father will have gone into a bookmaker and placed that type of bet. And whilst it might seem kinda sweet, this was not a £1 each way wager – maybe rugby player, maybe dancer, maybe artist, maybe scientist, maybe house-husband. Nope, this was an absolutely explicit expectation, a determined plan: mapping out the life of his boy who is obviously going to have to be good at sports – there is a lot of money at stake here.

And the dilemma for the woman was that the boy was not interested in sports, in fact, as he grew older he seemed to increasingly frustrate the father in his failure to be a proper boy and be good at proper boy stuff. The boy was intelligent and polite and impressed his teachers at school with his charm and good manners. The boy was caring and sensitive and seemed intuitively to recognise emotions in others. He was by all accounts a lovely lad. When he started to get picked on at school he didn't like to fight back, he didn't like fighting. He tried to tough it out and ignore the bullies, but school was getting increasingly unpleasant, one morning he just couldn't face it and feigned a poorly tummy to get out of going. His mum knew there was something wrong and finally got the boy to fess up. Later that day, when the father returned from work and found out his son was being picked on he got angry, very angry.

For the woman who now sat before me, telling the story was more than painful, and she wept as she described what had occurred. Initially, he taunted the boy for not fighting back, jabbing the boy with a fist in his chest but with increasing force until the boy could withhold his tears no longer. The boy started to cry.

"My son's a fucking sissy, a gay-boy, a fucking poof too frightened to stand up for himself, grow some fucking balls you poof", he was now screaming in the boy's face.

This young boy, aged barely seven at this point, stood there scared and humiliated before his father, believing he had failed in his father's eyes, frightened of his father's temper. He ran over and embraced his mother for comfort and protection but this just provoked the father further; added petrol to the fire of his rage that then exploded in a fireball of violence. Turning on his wife the man stood there, just inches from her face, this giant of a man physically dominated the scene as he towered over her, their frightened son nestled under her right arm. As his rage reached a crescendo the words lost individual meaning and became a blur of sound symbols that conveyed a palpable experience of hatred and desire for annihilation, the spit from his mouth stung her face like poisonous venom as she stood there terrified, frozen to the spot.

Time loses meaning on these occasions and she was not sure how long it had actually lasted, maybe just a few minutes, maybe less than a minute, she couldn't say but eventually the man had left the house and went to the pub, returning much later that evening, and long after the boy had gone to bed.

She came to see me, wondering if there was truth in her husband's assertion that she had turned her son gay. She blamed herself, she adored her boy and it was true that she did stand up for him against the father sometimes – but didn't think at the time she was being over-protective, now she found herself racked with guilt. She explained, she liked being with her son and as their only child took time to play with him; she liked the fact that her son would help her in the kitchen and together they often made cakes to decorate. The boy was already showing a natural talent and creative flare in the kitchen and she enjoyed having him with her doing the baking. But this activity did not earn appreciation or approval from the father who would dismiss any offerings, and then shout at the mother, telling her off for getting the boy 'doing sissy stuff'.

Clearly, being a top chef is just too gay. Perish the thought they might have the next Jamie Oliver or James Martin emerging from the apron strings of this apparently 'over-protective' mum. No, hopefully he'll be more interested in enjoying an activity that involves men in tight shorts chasing each other in turn and wrestling the nominated 'lucky guy' into the mud by grabbing his waist with a large hug, and sliding big powerful hands down his muscled muddy thighs while keeping your face pressed against his butt cheeks. Then when playtime is over, everyone gets to be naked in the bath together – oops, where's the soap. It's not like there is any homo-eroticism in Rugby, no, that's a real man's game.

Sardonic humour aside, for me the tragedy is that part of this hyper-masculine identity caught up in the same local sub-culture, is a clear rule that being 'one of the boys' involves regularly drinking to excess and when returning from a night out, nominated driver is the one who is least drunk – oh, and only a sissy wears a seat belt. Too many young lives have been lost in this stupidity, and this makes me angry. Really angry.

Ultimately, the real paradox here is that the desperate need to be seen as NOT GAY is correlated with proving how NOT LIKE A GIRL a guy is. It's an interesting naivety that assumes all gay men are effeminate – that effeminacy necessarily equates with homosexuality. And for the woman above, the reality was that her husband secretly viewed gay porn over the internet – this giant, muscular, tight t-shirt wearing rugby playing beer drinking man was aroused at the sight of male bodies. Crazy huh!

So, next time you see a car with the ubiquitous window sticker proclaiming 'Princess on board' or 'cheeky monkey on board' consider the rules and implicit expectations set out in the gendered identity that sits in the parent's mind and imagine how that might contrast with a way of being that could exist within a young person's mind if they had the freedom to be who they really want to be. When a parent innocently remarks they want 'one of each', ponder on what is the difference, what makes the difference significant? How might we all afford the next generation more freedom to define themselves by their own interests and not by a set of expectations dependant on apparent chromosomal inheritance?

Is it a boy or a girl? – yes, well yes and no.

On Being Transgender

"Karen who waited until she was forty-five to pursue full female attire, expresses self-identity this way:

"To use the more common terminology, I would say I am trans-gendered. I cross-dress but not for sexual display or attraction. There is a feeling that is feminine, pretty, and desirable. Yet, I don't change as a person. My gestures and walk are compatible with a feminine appearance, but not exaggerated, my voice unchanged, I don't consider myself a different person, just another visage or aspect of the same person My friends that observe me in both modes would substantiate this, In addition, passing is of no concern to me. I don't really 'do outreach' or 'in your face' but only subject myself to situations in which people are aware of my maleness. At times I prefer feminine gestures and expressions but more often masculine responses, When societal binarism insists I choose one pole or another, I choose masculine. I have been raised as a male, my sexual anatomy is male, etc. Nonetheless, I insist that I am ambigenderal. I claim all gender space, if you will, and exist within this spectrum at different points at different times."

(Bolin 1994, 464)

The evolution of a transgender identity.

When I was three going on four, my first best-est friend was the girl who lived next door. She was cool. Although I don't remember much from that time I know we played a lot together, and shared and swapped toys, even in adolescence I still had a toy she'd given me. Unfortunately we moved a lot when I was young so finding myself in a new town and starting a new primary school, meant finding a new best-est friend. This time it was another girl, called Catherine White. She was cool as well, and we spent hours talking to each other, much to the annoyance of the teacher who eventually sat us at her desk – where we continued to chat away to each other, way too much. She was a good friend to have.

And then, inevitably, and heartbreakingly, it was time to move again, this time up the educational hierarchy into junior school and this was where things started to really go awry. Suddenly there were boy gangs and girl groups and they occupied opposite ends of the school playground. Boys dissed each other, fought each other and ran around a lot. My best friend there was Mark who said that when he grew up he wanted to be a fairy: kinda cute for a lad of eight years of age. We mostly spent playtime digging holes in the tarmac of the playground with stones we found in the sports field. And it was here I guess that a growing awareness of gender difference set in - it was at junior school I properly learned that I didn't qualify or fit properly into the 'boy' group. I was intelligent (ie: a swot and therefore a poof and not a proper boy) and bad at sports (and therefore a poof and thus not a proper boy). I didn't in those days know what a poof actually was (except you could only be one if you were a boy but if you were one then that meant you weren't really a boy – work that out) but it obviously wasn't a helpful thing to be, since it involved people being horrible to you a lot of the time.

Being at school means facing certain harsh realities about your status in the world, and the potential for humiliation and rejection by the peer group is nowhere more evident than in the ritualised reiteration of social hierarchy played out in the activity known as 'picking teams' for school sports. Now, whilst being picked for team sports is an uncomfortable memory for many people, for me and my friend Mark it was more than painful. Week after week the teacher would select the two most popular boys and appoint them team captains to pick the teams for football. Mark and I would quip between us who would be picked last, I usually won. On one occasion as the opposite team picked Mark and I remained there in the former line-up, stood alone in front of my peers, the team captain suggested that perhaps the other team would like to have an extra player as he didn't want me in his team. Nothing was said.

If you wonder why I have such a thing against football I guess we can say a lot of the roots were back here. Team sports taught me nothing constructive about teams. I would be shoved in defence, not because I was good in defence, but because it got me out of the way to some inconsequential role. How might it have been, if different people got a turn at being team captain, at selecting a team based on the idea of people contributing their individual talent to the greater good? I don't suspect it is any different in schools today; another generation of children suffer the same humiliation in front of their peers with the collusion of the adults responsible for managing their welfare.

If primary school had introduced the first separation of the sexes into binaried groups, then secondary school reiterated and reinforced this with a new level of social panopticonic policing. This was a point at which I became really aware of being very much estranged from the girl group since although I wanted to mix with and join the girls, talking to girls would identify you as a sissy, not a 'proper boy', and therefore liable to being picked on: it was a dilemma. I was aware of my envy of the girls, I increasingly felt like I wanted to belong to the girl group – they just seemed nicer to be with. I started to imagine what it would be like to be one of them.

As we all started going through puberty and body shapes started changing, I became caught in a curious mix of adoration and envy as I noticed the shape of the girls as they filled out. Boys would make misogynistic remarks about 'wanting to shag the tits off' some girl or another. I just looked on enviously at them, admiring how they looked, the clothes they wore a clear demarcation of their group, and seeing them as desirable at both an erotic and an emotional level – here was a group of people whose characteristics I admired, they seemed nicer, more friendly, more collaborative and I was turned on by them and yet wanted to be one of them. It was a confusing time.

As we progressed through the 1970's a new fashion emerged as the A-line school skirt was replaced by the stitched down box-pleat and I remember the start of one autumn term as one of the more popular girls was first to have the new style. She looked amazing, the hip profile, the shape and movement of the skirt; the whole visual aesthetic was much more flattering to the average figure than the A-line and it wasn't long before they were the more common style. I was deeply jealous. Towards the end of the 1970's wool-mix tights increasingly replaced socks as part of girl's uniform and these held their own fascination – being very alien to anything available in boy-world. I was increasingly aware of the appeal of girl-only items of clothing – the things that had no equivalent in boy-world and that these were things I couldn't have access to; things I could never have: skirts, leotards, tights, tutus, puff-sleeve summer dresses. These identifiers of girl-world I increasingly coveted as symbols that would give me access to girl world, to identify me as belonging to the girl group and free me from the constraints of hegemonic masculinity tied up in boy-world.   Little wonder that with teenage hormones running amok they began to some extent to take on a unique excitement of their own, a partially eroticised frisson: symbolising the desired at both a sexual and an identificatory level.

So, as the two worlds diverged further through the journey of adolescence, I felt more confused and more isolated. Even then I wasn't naive enough to think that girls necessarily had it easy. I could recognise some of the social disadvantages girls faced in those days -this was the 1970's, and girls were seemingly destined to become typists or hairdressers until they married a man and settled down to become the next generation of housewives. Biology was destiny in those days for both sexes, in the absence of gender reassignment surgery (which hadn't featured on my radar at that time) for me it wasn't like there was any option anyway – I was a boy and I just had to get on with it.

And it wasn't that I didn't like some boy things. I loved making and fixing stuff, loved playing with Lego and Meccano; made Airfix kits; fixed my bike. I used to love playing down the municipal dump, clambering about the big metal containers of waste, raiding stuff from people's rubbish to take home and make things from. We were poor so I adopted the make and mend approach – figured if you want one, find a broken one and fix it – still guilty of that to this day. I liked helping dad fix the car – maybe because it helped me feel like a man because in my world growing up it was a way of proving my credentials as someone attempting to become a MAN. It was what real men did - fix cars and have dirty hands. It was also pretty much the only way to get time with dad anyway – that and helping him fix the house. Knowing how to fix cars and fix houses has always served me well too – and if girls don't get to use tools and fix stuff then that's a bit of a problem. See how confusing it gets when the rules about being male or female are constrained by such arbitrary delineators.

If it felt like the rules of the boy-group at school were being rigid and strictly policed then sadly home-life offered no let up. My mother didn't like girls, she had only wanted to have sons and was determined that we would fulfil her aspirations to be proper men. She made it clear that I had to be strong and competent and responsible and was to 'be the man of the house' when dad was at work – which was seemingly most of the time. Being scared or upset was not allowed and would be met with the mocking injunction 'what are you, man or mouse?' Only one answer was acceptable. Body posture, gait and movement were also policed with similar injunctions – 'walk like a man for goodness sake' and 'don't stand like that, it makes you look effeminate'. I once made the mistake of calling her 'mummy' (albeit I was only maybe eight or nine) – bad mistake, definitely not a boy thing to do. Toys and activities were similarly delineated – even eagle-eyed Action Man – the quintessential boy-toy of the 1970's was out of bounds since she had made it clear that we were not to play with dolls and that since action man was obviously a doll it was therefore not acceptable: only girls played with dolls.

We never had a dressing up box, and strangely, even at age five I already knew that dressing up was not a boy thing to do. I recall being invited to a friend's party where they had a pirate theme. One of the mums had burned the end of a cork and was smudging charcoal blacking onto the children's faces: I remember being deeply uncomfortable as this felt very childish and I needed to be a MAN – mum said. Messages from mum were powerful and simplistic and for a small boy learning about the world and learning about how to be in the world to a greater extent unquestionable. It was only later that some of those messages could be seen as the oftentimes somewhat bizarre rants of a woman who just couldn't cope and who had ultimately needed to parentify the eldest son to help her cope. In fairness, she had her own demons.

If she was determined that we would all turn out as proper MEN she also made it clear (somewhat confusingly) that she was against us showing aggression or hitting others, which meant that we were not allowed to stand up for ourselves at school by fighting back: and this meant not only being picked on a lot but also not properly belonging to the boy group since being good at fighting was a sin-qua-non of hegemonic masculinity. It was only towards the end of my school career that I learned that being prepared to hit the bully back very hard was ultimately the only solution to the problem when reason had failed. Kenny Rogers, the country and western singer put it neatly and uncomfortably in his song 'Coward of the County': much as I hate violence, sadly there is an ultimate truism that some people only understand very simple language - and sometimes you have to fight when you're a 'man'.

Of course, my mother may have had an ulterior motive in dissuading us from fighting back since her own aggression towards us would at times know no bounds, and I know that to some extent I acquired a degree of what the psychologist Martin Seligman describes as 'learned helplessness' as a legacy of the trauma of those early experiences. However, learning to stand up to bullies and fight back – whether physically or psychologically I ultimately learned to do, and I recognise this has been an important part of what makes it possible find and embrace the courage to come out - and be out - as transgender or gender-queer.   When you have a victim identity you inevitably stand out – I guess it's maybe an animal thing - like the lame wildebeest who is easily singled out from the herd and then becomes vulnerable to attack and annihilation. Certain kids at school just get picked on – later in life, as an adult and working in schools as a teacher I could more easily see how that came to be. As a child I just knew that other people were mostly dangerous, I was vulnerable to harm, and to the greater extent I just didn't fit in, especially within my peer group. I was desperate for acceptance, to fit in, but struggled to qualify, I was desperate to be a proper boy; I desperately needed to ensure I would become a proper man: the message to comply with the standards and meet the strict criteria for 'masculinity' was coming from all directions and the penalty for failure was not to be contemplated.

The one place I seemed to find acceptance was among the coach drivers who took us to school. They offered an exciting image of manhood – a proper man job, driving a big coach. There were four regular drivers, and they became like friendly uncles to chat to, one of them, Will, even had an HGV class 1 – he could drive artic lorries too. This much impressed the teenage boy who engaged them in conversation each day and took time to learn the names of the various coach types and classes, watching intently as the drivers operated the various controls. With the coaches sat in the car park, I'd be first out the door when the four o' clock bell rang and I'd be first on the coach, bagging the front seat and asking if I could sit in the driver position until it was time to go. Sitting there I could imagine how it would feel to drive one – this would be a proper male identity. One of the less regular drivers offered me the chance to come down to the yard and have a go at driving his coach for real. At thirteen I knew that probably wasn't allowed but he made the offer a few times and one day I cycled down to the yard where the coaches were stored to take up the offer. He wasn't there and I was disappointed but figured I'd have to try another day. I tried on a couple of other occasions but not long after that he stopped driving for the firm and I later heard that he had jumped in front of a train one night following allegations made against him by another pupil. It feels strange looking back on that time, my professional work now has led me to read up on research that suggested that paedophiles could identify vulnerability merely by looking at photographs of children: it's not that they would select the most physically attractive, no, they would consistently select the ones whose image, in some often very subtle ways, suggested weakness or vulnerability: as in nature, the predator seeks out wounded prey. I guess I was lucky.

At fifteen my first girlfriend was Sally-Ann. She was brill and having a girlfriend suddenly raised my profile within the boy group. Suddenly I had status, kudos. Suddenly, I qualified as a boy. All the lads who had been blagging about this girl and that became respectful that I had secured a girl where many of them had yet to despite all their bravado. Sally-Ann wore a blue knife-pleat school skirt and it was the first skirt I ever tried. We were alone in her house and she had gone to the kitchen to get a drink. I looked at it, slumped on the floor by the side of the bed, a combination of curiosity and temptation battled guilt and shame as I contemplated touching and maybe even wearing this almost sacred thing. In that fleeting moment, my heart pounding, temptation got the better of me and I suddenly found myself stood on her side of the bed, picking it up off the floor and nervously fumbling to try it on before she returned: I hadn't even fastened the zip before I was hurriedly taking it off in a combination of shame and terror and guilt. What had possessed me? I did not know but the priority was to avoid discovery so I made sure I put it back on the floor, scrumpled in exactly the same way she had left it. I remember feeling disgust with myself at the time. It felt very wrong.

I didn't succumb to temptation for some time after that.

At eighteen I was at university and living in a shared house. It was summer and a new fashion had hit the streets: the Ra-Ra skirt. Women's fashion seems to go in cycles between powerful and dynamic and then back to girly, flirtatious, coquettish. The Ra-Ra was the latter three, distinctly girly; almost diminutive since it echoed the frills of a small girl's dress; it was just adorable. And one of the girls in the house had one – a white three tier Ra-Ra, with alternate red and green ribbon piping: and one day it was there, in the corner of the bathroom floor. Now, one of the difficulties of being transgender and 'still in the closet' is that it is an identity that is easily shame based, and as a consequence of that, access to clothes necessarily becomes furtive and therefore additionally shame based. A vicious cycle is created that leads to further self-loathing and shame. It makes the whole experience fraught with tension, excitement; guilt and self-disgust. And that day, as I stood in the bathroom and looked at this beautiful skirt laying on the floor I weighed it up. The idea to try it on haunted my mind but I knew it would be wrong – disrespectful to the girl, perverted, disgusting, gross; completely unacceptable. And yet, with the bathroom door secured no-one would know, no-one would ever need know, I could know, I could know how it felt to wear this gorgeous skirt. I wrestled my conscience but knew a part of me really craved to experience the feel of it. Noting carefully how it was placed on the floor, observing and mentally mapping the way it had been cast down, the angle in which the waist-band was placed, how the corner of the hem leant slightly up the edge of the bath surround, the way it folded over itself: I carefully lifted it off the floor. I held it for a moment against my waist and then, a moment later I had tried it on. Suddenly, I was wearing it, I was actually wearing a skirt, I was actually wearing this skirt, this gorgeous Ra-Ra skirt - and it's a weird experience, an almost drug fuelled thrill of having given myself permission to try it, the actual experience of doing it when it went against all these internal taboos, and then the struggle to create the illusion in my mind, to imagine that it had now transformed me into the girl I wanted to be. I looked down at my lower body, the skirt draped slightly incongruently on my narrow hips, the waist fitted but my hips didn't fill it out to create the proper fall. The tiers were so pretty but knobbly kneed hairy legs emerged from it and it just looked wrong. Wrong, wrong, wrong – I was mentally beating myself up. I wanted to imagine smooth girl legs emerging from the hemline of this gorgeous skirt, what I saw however, looked ridiculous; and in that moment the spell was broken and the skirt was quickly removed and placed immediately but carefully back on the bathroom floor, exactly as it had been before.

Once again I had let the genie out of the bottle, experienced the forbidden, and then been overcome by the associated guilt, shame and self-disgust that had me putting it firmly back in the bottle and ramming the cork down further and harder. And it was therefore going to be some time before I made any further forays into girl world.

Towards the end of the second year of university I recognised that going to Uni had been the wrong choice, for the wrong reasons, at the wrong time, and ultimately it would always be the wrong course for me; so despite the inevitable aggro dropping out was going to accrue I dropped out. And it did accrue aggro but hey, I'd become accustomed to aggro so nothing new there then. So I found myself leaving Scotland and heading south of the border to find work – ending up in Oxford where the job centre actually had some jobs.

I secured a job at the boat yard and was there, painting the hire fleet and learning how to fix and build boats. I kept my 'girl-self' repressed for a while and passed quite successfully as male – I was doing a proper man's job – manual work that involved getting my hands dirty and covered in cuts and grazes, wearing an oily boiler suit covered in the grime of an engine bay, wearing army boots with steel toecaps: all very manly. And then I met the girl who would ultimately become my first wife.

She was very pretty truth be told, and she wore lovely clothes. For me, I was hoping the whole 'wanting to be a girl' thing would go away; maybe it was just a phase. Surely I'd grow out of it, especially if I had a girlfriend and was married and such, and therefore could finally prove I could be a proper BLOKE. I guess I thought it would make me somehow FEEL like a proper man, which I was hoping did not involve wanting to be a woman or wear women's clothes. Finally I could be normal and just get on with my life, free of the hidden shame. I was wrong. What it actually did was give me easy access to a wardrobe filled with temptation and a selection of outfits in size 10-12. And wouldn't ya just know it, that's my size too! D'oh. So, if for the intervening couple of years the genie had been securely contained in the bottle, now, once again temptation was getting the better of me and I was raiding her clothes rail whenever she was out. Don't get me wrong here, I hated the idea of the deception, it did feel a little disrespectful but how else would I get girl clothes to wear – it wasn't exactly like I could go to a shop and get my own. I mean, how could I?

One day, finally the secret came out and as I feared there was disapproval. The deal was that if I wanted to wear a skirt I had to go buy my own and not steal hers. Fair enough. And so, I went to town to buy my first skirt.

Call me kitsch if you like but we are talking 1980's here. Laura Ashley did the most adorable long flared corduroy skirt (look cord was fashionable back then ok) so that was tempting, but Monsoon had opened in Oxford high street and had the most amazing clothes. I found myself heading to Monsoon for my first shopping expedition. And then I have to build up the courage to go in, thinking about how to avoid exposure. I have to create a cover story. Yes, I'm buying this for my girlfriend, a present. 'She's size 10-12 I think'. I've rehearsed it and I have my cover. My heart pounding I think I'd have been less scared if I'd gone out shoplifting instead – maybe there is less to be ashamed off – figure having to admit actually the skirt is for me. Way too scary. Anyway, I walk in and note the skirt is still on the same rail. I've done my reconnaissance you see, when we were last in town together I made some mental notes - noted the positions, the locations and had been preparing this mission with almost SAS precision – I even knew how much it was and had the correct cash sitting in my pocket ready to make the transaction swift. Straight in, get the skirt, pay for it, straight out without raising suspicion. The plan works like clockwork and walking home with my monsoon bag feels quite elating. I've done it, bought my first skirt. It was perfect, really pretty, a really full skirt with a really nice semi-basque detail at the top. I get it home and the celebration is short lived as a new reality sets in. As I describe earlier in the book, despite it being her idea that I have my own skirt, my wife finds it's hard to get her head around the whole girl-mode thing and out of respect for her I mostly only opted to wear it when she was out and I was alone. My sense of shame and defectiveness were compounded ultimately by her rejection of me expressing my femininity in such a way. I understand it was hard for her – I guess she didn't know what she was getting when we got together – it's not normally the first thing you 'fess up. And I honestly believed the whole dressing up thing would go away – that having a girlfriend would make me 'normal'. And anyway, imagine – boy meets girl and it's love at first sight and the guy says "OMG, simply love your outfit, if we go out together can I get to borrow it". I don't think so.

So, a couple of years later and I've left the boatyard and started doing general building. Very blokey, very masculine – just like a REAL MAN. I have dirty dusty clothes and chunky boots and rough calloused hands. I can feel like a man doing this work, the outward image of myself passes quite convincingly as male: even if I'm wearing tights under my jeans. What, you say? In fairness, although my wife continued to be uncomfortable with the whole skirt situation she did think it was a good idea to wear woollen tights in the winter to protect my knees and joints from the cold, so with her encouragement I was able to wear tights – ribbed woollen ones (not sheer of course) because lots of men working in cold environments do, you know, fishermen and builders and bikers, so that's ok then.

Anyway, I find myself working on a contract in Glasgow so I'm working away from home for two weeks. Staying in a flat while I renovate the kitchen. I'm on my own albeit a labourer is booked to help me in the daytime. A few doors down the road is an Indian clothes shop. The shop is a classic hippy emporium filled with incense, beads, crystals, and of course, beautiful hippy clothes. There's a really cute little flared miniskirt in Indian print cotton and it hangs enticingly on the end of a rail visible from the window. I walk past the shop each night on the way to the chippy to get my fish supper. The skirt draws me to the window each time I pass and once again I am wrestling my conscience – the guilt and shame that tells me that cross-dressing is such a perverted thing to be doing and the part of me that is desperate to just wear the bloody thing and enjoy it. It's totally the perfect opportunity though – no-one knows me here, I won't be sticking around beyond the contract; and in the evenings I'm staying in the flat alone. By close of play on the third day the skirt is mine and I treat myself to a long soak in the bath while eating my fish supper and drinking a can of beer (that must be my girl brain doing the multi-tasking) before finally getting to spend the remainder of the evening wearing it and enjoying it. The hairy leg problem solved of course by the wearing of thick ribbed woollen tights, which actually made the whole visual aesthetic work better as my legs seemed smoother, less knobbly, less spindly.

That couple of weeks allowed me for the first time to begin to properly relax and enjoy wearing a skirt without fearing discovery or exposure. At home I had to ensure all the curtains were drawn before getting changed which in daytime is not only depressing but suspicious too. Here, the flat was above street level, no-one could look in: here, behind the locked door of this first floor flat I was safe and here, wearing this skirt just felt so natural and good. Taking off my builders' clothes at the end of the day and putting on clean tights, my skirt and a pullover and mooching round the flat, sitting watching telly; drinking a can of beer; eating a fish supper. It just felt natural; it felt comfortable and I see what people mean by the idea of using cross-dressing as a form of relaxation. It felt very comfortable to be doing this. Sadly though, the opportunity afforded by this situation would be short lived and with the job completed on schedule, it was not long before it was time to head home and back to reality. The skirt went in my bag and came home with me although there were few occasions to enjoy the same freedom, the same sense of enjoyment and liberation.

For any number of somewhat tragic reasons, the cross-dressing probably being the lesser of many, after eight years my wife and I parted company. I moved out and in a classic purging episode disposed of all my girl clothes. Asides from the two skirts already mentioned, I had also acquired a few other pieces over the years: but I was determined that I would not take that legacy to the next relationship. It was not going to be acceptable so it needed to be disposed of. Surely throwing away the clothes would fix the problem. I convinced myself that a fresh start would finally resolve the situation. And this time my new girlfriend, lovely as she was, took a size 16 – so not my size. And in any case she didn't really do girly-girl clothes. Surely problem solved. And for a few years the whole wanting to be a girl thing remained repressed as I struggled to make a living and change career and do humungous amounts of commuting. They were hard years albeit there were times when we had fun. She was keen on folk dance and since she was useless on a sewing machine I took the opportunity to make the dance costumes for her – a vicarious cross-dressing experience as I imagined what it would feel like to be wearing them. Hers of course wouldn't fit me so no point trying. I resisted the temptation to buy any girl clothes during my time with her although I did stick with the woolly tights as riding the motorbike in winter made them an absolute essential.

When we reached a point where we had to go our separate ways I took the time to be single and at that point started to once again amass a few items of girl clothing. I ordered some underwear from a catalogue and started wearing women's underwear full time. One day while in town and checking out the charity shops I spotted a pleated girl's games skirt hanging on the end of the row. I simply had to have it – it had a 30″ waist – it couldn't have been more perfect, it was one of those classic icons of girl identity and for a long time it remained a favourite as I found that it not only fitted me nicely, it actually hung quite well despite my lack of hips.

Buying things in shops was still quite furtive and I would make the most of Christmas and Valentines day to act as cover story especially if it was lingerie I was buying – the ol' present for my GIRLFRIEND cover story. Yeah, bet they've not heard that one before.

In the intervening period, as I took time out of relationships to work out what I wanted I also tried to make sense of this need to wear female clothing. I tried reading books on the phenomenon of transsexualism, tried to find out the causes of cross-dressing and transvestism. Surely if there was a cause there was a cure! This of course turns out to be a fool's mission although the exploration was interesting. Cross-gendered identities just are - the pathology is society's, not the poor soul who just wants the freedom to identify with a group of people that seem to have more in common than the group previously assigned. However, the books I was finding and reading at the time confused me (and remember this is still too early for the Internet). I really struggled to work out where I was in the whole equation. At that time it seemed like there were two options: either I was apparently some pervert getting sexual kicks off the clothes and afflicted with 'transvestic fetish' or some tragic soul who always knew he was trapped in the wrong body and just needed some surgery to fix the problem. Once again I didn't seemingly fit into a narrowly defined binary. I wasn't properly boy or girl; I wasn't even proper transvestite or transsexual. Obviously, transsexual was the closer fit but since I wasn't entirely sure I wanted to do the whole surgery thing (and apparently transsexuals always knew) maybe that ruled me out. Also, I could recognise that I didn't properly qualify as a transsexual as it seemed you needed to always just do girl things and not like boy things. I kinda did both so that seemed to rule me out. And it seemed to be a proper transsexual meant you couldn't be attracted to women as 'obviously' lesbian transsexuals had yet to be invented. So I was confused. There was another element at this time to the exploration of my cross-gendered identity that caused me confusion and was contaminated by these archaic and pathologising paradigms.

I wanted to experience myself as female – and yet the identifiers of femininity were for me, primarily or initially caught up in stereotypical iconography – dressing as a schoolgirl; bridesmaid; ballerina. It's easy to pathologise and pejoratively think of these identities as merely fetish enactment and maybe for some they are; but in my case it was much deeper, more meaningful. Trying these identities allowed me a chance to finally experience and physically explore the meaning of these early images – identities that had been denied me: identities and ways of being that had been deeply and longingly envied and coveted from my earliest memories. It's almost as if the process of self actualisation, of growth and the development of a congruent transgender identity necessarily involved a brief visit through the key stages of girlhood before allowing a more grown up feminised identity. Curiously, dressing up is an activity that we encourage in children, but how is it that girls are allowed to do it more so than boys and to a much older age? A storm erupted this week on the Internet over an American mother who allowed her five year old son to go to a Halloween party as his favourite television character, Daphne from Scooby-Doo. And the problem here was that two of the mothers at school took issue with her over this thinking that she would TURN HER SON GAY! This of course suggested they not only believed that this is actually possible but also that being gay would be a bad or unacceptable thing. Wrong on three counts - the third being the naive and erroneous assumption that being effeminate and/or female identified necessarily means sexually attracted to men and therefore gay – it's back to the simplicity of the culturally reiterated heterosexual matrix. The woman's blog (Cops Wife 2010) makes an intelligent defence of her actions and tells the story in full to set the context.

Encouraging children to do 'dressing up' is seen as educational, developmentally beneficial and ultimately about allowing them to experience other worlds through a process of identification and role-play. And yet, it would appear from the clinical texts as if an adult who does the same is to be considered perverted or disordered unless it's in the context of a drunken party – and now amuse yourself with this thought: ponder why it is that the average rugby club fancy dress party typically involves at least half the team coming as either tarts or schoolgirls. I guess it's not like your average uber-macho rugby player ever wondered what it was like to be feminine. N'ah.

Ultimately, I knew that deep down this need to wear women's clothes was a very fundamental part of who I was, I knew I didn't dress up for some apparently 'bizarre' sexual kink, I knew that the desire to wear female clothes was about identifying the female aspects of myself. As I allowed myself to experience wearing female clothes more often they became more natural; I reconnected to the feeling of freedom I'd found back in the flat in Glasgow all those years ago. I enjoyed how I felt when dressing in grrl-mode. And women's clothes often have a different feel so the experience of the body becomes different, the textures of the fabrics, the fall and movement. It's a different experience physically, emotionally, psychologically: I'd experienced liberation, and yet I still felt overwhelmingly constrained and ultimately confined by the combination of internalised shame and societal pressure to conform to only have male identified clothes and this was just so depressing.

I found myself struggling to know what to do, to work out how to be – whether to allow myself to buy female clothes, let myself wear them at home albeit behind closed curtains, or rid myself of them and make a more concerted effort to be a proper male, to be rid of this damned affliction. I'd given the former strategy a bit of a go but was finding I'd been getting increasingly angry around this time, angry about a lot of things, angry at myself especially. My hair which I'd had long for years had finally got too thin and had now been cut very short, I mourned and resented the loss but turned the hurt into more anger and concluded I needed to give myself a boot up the backside and stop all this 'feminine-side' nonsense: so I purged the wardrobe again, grew a beard and decided to become a proper man for once and for all.

To that end, I decided I needed to make more of an effort to understand how to think 'male' so I joined an off-roading club and started buying lad's mag –'FHM', which in fairness was the least pornographic and dare I say, more intelligent of a new genre of male interest printed media. And lad's mags were part of a rising zeitgeist supposedly promoting the new male identity for the 1990's. I think that the editors at FHM were trying to create a Cosmo for guys. I gave it a go, I tried to understand how I was supposed to feel as 'a man', to try and like what I was supposed to like – but in truth, if I was depressed at the idea of having to let go of being a girl and become a proper man, then what I read about how to be a proper man was even more depressing. Each month's edition just painted a picture of how sorry masculinity really is as an identity and I just couldn't say I wanted to aspire to this. As for the off-roading club – they were nice enough as lads go but they were lads, and I just didn't think like them or want to really get involved in some of the escapades they were engaging in. Eventually, I gave up on both counts and started buying female clothes again.

Creating a feminine body image is an interesting phenomenon in itself. The mind imagines a female self; the eyes see a male self and the illusion is broken. There are so many physical variations beyond genitalia that betray a chromosomal inheritance. And don't imagine it's as simple as acquiring pair of false boobs, a bit of hip padding, and some heavy foundation to mask the beard shadow that will make up the difference. To the human eye there are many subtle differences – the shape of the face, the jaw, the cheek bones, the space between the eyes, the shape of the eye sockets, the shape of eyebrows, the hands, the shape of the legs, the space between the legs, the shape of the rib cage, the space between waist and hip, even the shape of the head. And then you have to consider the way the body moves, the gait, that stance, even the way the arm is used when walking. And that's before the illusion is completely shattered by seeing a pair of hairy arms emerging from the [sic]'adorable satin puff sleeves of a peach coloured bride's maid gown'. So creating a female body, or body-femaling involves relearning how to move, to stand, to interact physically in the world as well as recognising the limitations of genetic inheritance. And then there is the issue of hair removal.

I remember the first time I shaved my legs. And it was legs I did first. I wanted to look down at my body and start to feel as if it could communicate back femaleness. Everyone knows that so called 'tucking' is a sin-qua-non if, as a biologically in tact male, you are going to imagine a female lower torso - but hairy legs is a massive no-no. So, knowing that no one was going to get to find out before I had a chance for it to grow back I sat in the bath one night and shaved my legs. And it was a remarkably liberating and thrilling thing to do. They still lacked the smoothness and slender taper of proper girl legs but they at least were not afflicted by masculinising dark hair – it was a good compromise. And it felt good; the skin had a different feel and wearing tights even felt different, silkier, with the advantage that they actually looked better in a pair of ordinary tights – the blemishes and scars hidden by 40 denier mesh. I kept them like that for a few months, occasionally having to let up for a bit to deal with in growing hairs but mostly keeping them smooth. After a while the thought of shaving my arms increasingly intruded. This was clearly a step too far – the risk of discovery way too high – what if I was at work and forgot and rolled up my sleeves. Even in winter there were times when I might inadvertently roll up my sleeves. I imagined that people would notice and then there would be AWKWARD QUESTIONS to answer. One day I just did it. Shaved my arms. And it felt great. And I kept my sleeves down and got away with it. That said, there was one occasion when a particularly keen eyed pupil noticed my hands as hairless, and asked if I'd shaved them so I made a cover story about catching them in the flame of the brazing hearth and burning the hairs off. They knew me well enough to believe that was actually distinctly probable.

Over time I came to discover better technologies for hair removal – to each their own I guess, but for me the epilator works really well once you get used to the pain of the first two or three attempts. After that I think the hair gets weaker and finer and it's less painful when it's being yanked out by rotating ceramic discs whizzing past them.

During this period I experimented with various types of padding to create a more female profile. A major problem of buying female clothes and putting them on a biologically male body is to the greater extent they just don't fit. Obviously, if you want boobs you're gonna need some filler there, but even skirts and dresses are built around the female ideal of seventy-five percent ratio of waist to hip and for a slim male that's closer to ninety percent without corset or padding. I tried making my own with varying degree of success, tried buying off the Internet – again with varying degrees of success. What I found is that it is possible to create a reasonably 'convincing' female form but as Vicky Lee describes – it feels like being a trussed chicken. It just didn't feel real or comfortable so whilst the mirror could perform back an image that wasn't entirely unconvincing, inside the incredulity remained palpable.

At this stage, I still struggled to fully let myself go and would stop shy of using make-up. I've never been a fan of lipstick and anyway my thing has always been for girls with big dark eyes. So, whilst well applied eye-make up does it for me I'd never been a fan of the pancake foundation or bright red lipstick you tend to see on the moving dolls staffing the typical department store make-up counter. Yeuigh. But for my part, at this stage I wasn't even ready to use moisturiser let alone make-up! I still had some journey to travel before these became possible.

After a while, I found myself in a new relationship and took the opportunity to fess up to the whole dressing up thing straight away. At that time I contained my forays into girl world strictly behind closed doors (and curtains) but had accepted that it was not going to go away and burning the wardrobe; getting a girlfriend, even growing a beard was still not going to turn me into a 'PROPER MAN' and therefore stop me wanting to wear girl stuff. It was a lost cause so I made it clear from the outset it was something I did. Gradually though, as I became more self-accepting, I found myself increasingly resentful of the pressure to hide away. Slowly I found myself wanting validation from the outside world of a true identity that yes, embraced feminine aspects.

Now, the performance of a feminine self is implicitly denoted by certain key-identifiers. On a typical day now, I wear girl's jeans, girl's pullover or top, coloured scarf, girl's boots, tights, and quite often a bit of light make-up (some days more than others). For many it goes under the radar since few read the jeans and jumper as 'obviously' women's-wear. There's a degree of androgyny in a jeans and jumper combo anyway, and whilst most articles of clothing are available to women these days, certain aspects of clothing have been denoted as exclusively female and or quintessentially female and thereby denied to men: the skirt is probably the most significant and overt of these and it's the one that seems to cross the biggest taboo.

At that time in my journey, I figured that maybe buying a kilt would be a more acceptable way to cross the line without crossing the line so to speak; wear a skirt without wearing a skirt; be out without blowing my cover and having to come out. My own clan tartan is not that inspiring so I decided to see what possibilities eBay offered and it wasn't long before I spotted a Black Watch kilt in my size -so I bought it. The great thing with eBay of course is the degree of anonymity it affords. A few days later the kilt arrived and then it was just a case of acquiring a thick leather belt to go with it. Now, if you've never actually worn a genuine Scots kilt before let me tell you they feel rather odd. Bulky is the first word that springs to mind. There is a lot of material in a kilt and the thing is very thick and, well, bulky – strangely it felt very different to wearing a skirt, hard as that might be to make sense of.

I wore it a couple of times at home with my partner present and then an opportunity to be 'out' in it arose. We were having a party at the house and so I chose this occasion to wear my kilt for the first time – in public. Paired with thick boot socks, heavy boots and a check shirt and proper belt it looked masculine – rather Mel Gibson in highlander. It raised a few comments but I got away with it. I had mixed feelings – mostly slight embarrassment, it had been ok, but I still felt ill at ease, unsure. I tried wearing it out again but still felt very self-conscious, odd even; so don't recall wearing it since. It was a useful experiment though.

Over a period of time as my research started to introduce me to new constructs such as gender-fuck; gender blending and the construct of 'transgender' as new ways of defining the gendered self, suddenly I had a model that would fit. I had a paradigm to explain something I'd been trying to make sense of for forty years. There was a new sense of potential, of growth, of self-actualisation available. New healthy ways of being gender-queer, of presenting both male and female aspects in ways that were honest and truthful became possible. I started to develop more awareness of how real women were, observing the extraordinary range of shapes and profiles and starting to note fashion elements and cuts that worked with certain body shapes and attributes. I realised that some chromosomal women also had no hips and bum; some had no boobs. I didn't need to have a perfect woman body – nobody did. Or like a lot of women, when I thought I saw someone who did, I was envious. That's the 'real girl' experience; never being happy with your body, always comparing it to others and finding it lacking in some way. Get with the program girl-friend!

I noted how women moved; there are many subtle movements that one can read at some distance. Learning those movements, those postures allowed me to inhabit my body in feminine ways, gave ways for my body to communicate back femaleness. Being female is a state of mind. I didn't want to pretend to be 'a woman' but wanted to find a look that would communicate that femaleness and explored ways of queering my gender presentation. And then the challenge was to find a wardrobe that would work – an authentic transgender wardrobe.

I had a favourite denim miniskirt that I loved the shape of but was frustrated by the poor fit. So I took it apart, modified the pattern and made a new one, which fitted much better and didn't need padding to hang properly. This gave me a skirt that hung well, fitted properly, moved nicely. Re-tailoring clothes to fit my body has given me a way of feeling more genuine – taking in the hips will make a skirt fit better if it's fitted and allow the flare of the skirt to hang better. Finding clothes to suit my shape is no different to any other woman – there are clothes we'd love to wear that just don't work with what nature gave us. The trick is to experiment and go with what looks good.

Ultimately, the biggest block to me embracing a transgender identity was the fear of being thought of as gay. I hadn't recognised it in myself, that I had my own homophobia, so subtle was the process. As a modern, liberal and free thinking post feminist I liked to think I was cool with homosexuality and the idea of people being gay. But, as I describe in an earlier chapter, when I was challenged by a colleague – would I be seen reading a copy of gay times while sat on a train or in a coffer bar my automatic answer revealed the problem – no, someone might think I was gay! This insight gave me the chance to work through the issues I still had about what being gay meant and finally allowed me to let go of that anxiety. Looking back at school days the origins were very clear – one day calling someone poof or queer or gay as an insult will be as outdated as the racist language we used so freely in the 1970's. That time has yet to come although I notice the current legislation building on the 'every child matters' campaign is heading in that direction.

Today, if I am out in my skinny black jeans and Uggs, wearing a pink scarf and a bit of light make-up, if someone reads me as transgender then well done them, if they think I'm 'gay' or a 'poof' then so long as they leave that thought in their head and let me go about my business then that's just fine. And to the greater extent it is.

What I find when I am out and about doing a more overt 'grrl-mode' with the hair and the skirt and very overtly trans, is that so long as I feel good about myself and have a smile of inner confidence, then, for the most part women smile at me, men ignore me. I like it that way.

Final thoughts

As part of my research for this book I recently visited a transgender festival in Manchester – the Sparkle event. It's the second time I've attended and here is where the beautiful, the weird, the wonderful, and the exotic get to parade in a festival that celebrates a freedom for the weekend to present a re-gendered self. There are numerous and varied presentations of transgender identities in all their forms, and particularly so 'male-femaling' where one can observe the full spectrum: from the satin and frill encased 'Shirley Temple' to the PVC clad 'Grace Jones'. It's an amazing experience being there, and as one of the few people with a beard it was interesting to wonder how I was being read.

Here I was struck by the variety of presentations and explanations people made for their way of being. What I did come away with was a sense that for many people who are transgender but unaware of the term (or the potential that the identity offers) that maybe they were left to self define in potentially outmoded and simplistic constructs, such as 'transvestite or transsexual'. I make the point earlier in the book that when Grayson Perry, the artist came across a copy of the News of the World, he discovered that what he was doing when he dressed up was apparently called 'transvestism'. And yet his version of 'transvestism' is very different say to Eddie Izzard. We must remember that previous conceptualisations have been framed within the constructs of hetero-normativity and therefore become defined as pathological because they sit outside the accepted norm. But the defining of 'norm' is questionable – what makes different necessarily 'abnormal' for example. No one asks what causes heterosexuality; for all the researchers looking for a gay gene, few seek to explain how sexual attraction is formed – why certain physical forms and types are desirable. It's not as if having the hetero-sexual gene would make someone attracted to all body types and appearances – our sexual desire is often quite specific. The understanding therefore of gendered ways of being has been caught up in the patriarchy of science and politics, and the implicit and very real disadvantage experienced by the repressed 'other'. So, women dressing as men would be seen as trading up and therefore easily understood (even if it missed the point) but why would a man want to be a woman, or be taken for a woman when it carried so much social disadvantage – the only logical answer it seemed back then was as a justification to have sex with other men.

From a historical perspective we can see some logic in this since men having sex with other men had been proscribed from the late 1700's onwards there may have been some truth in this idea in some cases – for the gay man back then being convicted of sodomy was a capital offence so the conversion to a female identity albeit for a visit to the local molly house would be a sin-qua-non for survival as we still see today in places like Iran. However, this does not explain by any means all men who want to dress as women and the idea I have wanted to convey in this book is that some men may have self identified with a construct that is still caught up in and contaminated by the cultural homophobia and misogyny that had been part of their formative histories and ultimately so endemic up to now within western society. There is a new generation emerging however who are enjoying new freedoms in terms of their sexuality, who may not face these same struggles. I say good luck to them.

For the wanna-be transsexual then, I pose the following question: If you were to wake up tomorrow with the body and wardrobe of a woman, what difference would you note in your life? Actually, it's an interesting question for all of us to ask. I reflect on a passage I read in Ekins (1997)

"Since being widowed in his 60's Ben/Dierdre is Ben outside his home and Dierdre inside it......Dierdre has her own personality, and 'femme' style quite separate from Ben. She is she explains 'a much nicer person than Ben, more tolerant, more forgiving. Dierdre enjoys sewing and homemaking; Ben enjoys cars...As Dierdre potters around the house doing the housework she finds herself thinking –I must wash Ben's socks" Ekins(1997:p19)

I find tremendous sadness in reading that passage – it seems like a very split identity, very dissonant and I ponder on the context that creates the need to be so un-integrated. There is a sense of role play in the Dierdre character but more tragic is the idea that core aspects of self, genuine and true personality traits are unavailable to each through some simplistic binaried rule set, necessitating the splitting of self, the disintegration of the true self. I note that Ben is involved in his local church and wonder if narrow religious doctrine may have a part to play here.

When I reflect on the question posed above, to imagine myself waking up as a woman, to have a woman's body, I find myself caught up in certain realities – that whilst in some ways it would seem like a dream come true, as in the best tradition of the fairy tale it would also be a case of be careful what you wish for – there's always a down side, not least of which is what sort of body I might end up with. And I can think of ways in which my life might be disadvantaged by being female in the magic-wand overnight conversion proposed above. There would be loss to contend with.

And I am aware that I would have no back history – I don't have the experience of being a girl in the playground, the young woman at university, the adult woman at work. So, even with the body I would be lacking significant elements of my identity – how does it feel to be a woman? Taking a systemic approach for a moment we might think that there is no such thing as feeling like a 'woman', only the experience of being a person, part of whose system was defined at key stages in their lives by the experiencing of others as them as female. And I don't have that. So, if I say that today I feel like doing I'm doing grrl-mode – what do I mean? Well, maybe I look a bit girl but not in an "in-your-face-I'm-a-laydee" type way. I've got my lush new Ugg boots, which are well cute, my tassled scarf and my skinny black jeans. In fact everything I am wearing is from a "woman's" wardrobe. I'm wearing a little foundation and have touched the corner of my eyes with the eyeliner and a dab of dark shadow to give a hint of roundness – so yep, wearing make-up and girl clothes- but I don't look like a transvestite thank goodness. I think this has been a big part of the mission. How to embrace the essence of a queered identity without pretending to 'be a woman' or creating a grotesque of stereotypical and over-idealised femininity? And this feels good; I can even allow myself to kind of move in a more girl way, articulating from the hips, holding my arm out to the side. I came across the following quote and found it connected for me, mirrored my sentiment:

"In my experience, Transpeople tend to become much more comfortable in their lives when they stop focussing on 'passing', realising that even passing convincingly is no guarantee for qualifying as a man or a woman. They may still have to deal with endless confrontation about why they are not 'genuinely' male or female - for example because they cannot have children. There are a great variety of transgender people who in some stereotypical view may not 'pass' but who feel so thoroughly at ease within themselves that nobody is going to argue. They may not 'pass' but they do 'convince'! The issue is not primarily one of being male female or neither but of being considered, respected and treated as whatever one experiences oneself to be"
Zandvleit, T. (in Neal & Davies 2000: p182)

So, it's a dilemma, lets face it - if I could 'pass' as a convincing woman then I guess it might seem as if life would be a load easier. Imagine I could emerge from the front door and be completely read and thought of as a biological woman, without hint of a doubt. Well of course, we might question where is the doubt, what is it that gives the game away? Well, even if I finessed the physical constraints, got the whole padding, wig, boobs, voice, movement sorted, there would still be so many other small cues that would give the game away. I think I'm still a little envious of the few who were gifted the characteristically feminine features that make the presentation as woman easier. I may be small framed, delicate boned but too many other cues offer the potential to be read and the philosophy I have come to increasingly adopt here is that 'passing' is still about presenting a false self to the world – so I'd be swapping one mis-read self for another and endlessly anticipating exposure. And that anxiety about exposure, that self-consciousness creates a tension that others can read. So that even a perfect presentation would be derailed by an inner doubt. Humans are animals and animals read vulnerability, and the sense of vulnerability comes from within – in this case from the fear of exposure.

And so then, by embracing the notion of a congruent Transgender identity, I come to a position that realises a new potential - that in finding a way to self accept, I can present a congruent self to the world and in that space let go of much of the inner doubt. Now there is no risk of exposure, I am me and here I am – you read me as transgender, between genders, biologically one, spiritually other, and here with you as both. I know as I write this that for some the philosophies and ideas in this book are challenging, uncomfortable perhaps even controversial in places, and yet these are only ideas, this is the sense I have made of the journey of exploration and discovery. I come to a conclusion in my mind that the problem with 'cross-dressing' and 'transvestism' in the classic sense is two-fold: I think the first problem is one of feared rejection – hence the associated shame and perceived need to live a secretive life. The second, a function of the first, is resolving the problem by attempting to 'pass' as other: however nobody likes being conned, being made to feel stupid for accepting a false presentation as real. And I think that applies to both male and female in as much as if the person before us pretends to be other and we are required to collude with that deception then that creates an internal tension which is easiest avoided. At a conference in Cardiff earlier this year, I presented as transgender in skinny jeans, Ugg boots, jewellery, make-up and long hair (and my lush parrot feather earrings) and found easy acceptance by the group with people interacting freely with me and asking questions openly. And yet, also in the conference, there was someone who presented as 'woman' but lacked the credibility and was clearly transgender.   Her uneasiness and the group's uneasiness created an isolation and she ended up drinking coffee alone at the interval. I went over to break the ice, a question about where she had come from. The transaction passed briefly, she chose not to comment on my transgender presentation and I didn't want to 'blow her cover' by suggesting she was anything other than as she asked to be read. It just felt too taboo and even now I feel sad about a lost opportunity.

Being 'out' as transgender has on the whole proved easier than I imagined although it is still necessary to risk assess the situation. I find the best way of achieving this is to simply ask myself, would a young single woman be out in this situation; how would she fare? It's a useful litmus test and seems to work effectively. Probably the biggest complication I experience arises as a result of the kind of fragility that can exist within (lesser) male identities: here I am thinking chiefly of the boys and men of lower socio-economic and or educational status, whose fragile male self is bolstered by the:

"deployment and performance of aggression, sexism, and homophobia."
Martino & Pallotta-Chiarolli (2003: p108)

It's as if, transported back to the school playground their definition of self needs to bolstered by in-vivo comparison to this childlike hegemonic ideal – men have to be strong and tough and courageous and not like girls, who are effeminate and therefore lesser than them: in the process of performing to the peer group the fragile male asserts he is 'more manly' than you because he can threaten you and in the process of pointing out your effeminacy and implicit inadequacy to the group, allows them to see that he is effectively more of a man than you. Ok – but who has the balls to be themselves, to have the courage to go out wearing make-up and a skirt – bet you aren't that brave. Now who's the 'man'?

Albeit politically convenient to separate the two, I assert slightly controversially here that to the greater degree, the issue of transphobia is essentially one of homophobia – that if people were not afraid of being gay, of being thought of as gay (and here regardless of whether actually they were or weren't homo or bisexual) then maybe people who blurred the gender lines would not pose such a threat – that to the greater extent transphobia only exists in the context of homophobia. If you solve the latter you might go a long way to solving the former.

I recall living through the 1980's and being very much aware of a new vibe. Homosexuality had come out of the closet and famous people like Elton John and Freddie Mercury, had come out as gay. Society was slowly starting to accept that the idea that people could be gay albeit with a, 'as long as they keep it to themselves' mentality. Living through that time taught me that although it takes time, the pioneering efforts of the few can inspire the many, and through that process eventually enough momentum can be built up to secure a fundamental change in the cultural milieu. In my lifetime I have seen societal mores changing in the domains of racism, sexism and homosexuality although I acknowledge there is still much to be done, I'd say we have come a long way from the dark ages of the 1970's. It is my belief that transgender identities can come out of the closet and become understood and ultimately accepted if enough momentum can be created.

Perhaps the biggest challenge to changing the prevalent zeitgeist surrounding transgender identities remains caught up in the historical language and conceptualisations. Cross-dressing and transvestism are words that in a sense name and shame. By their very existence they essentially create a problem by naming a phenomenon and defining it as 'other', by explicitly creating a pathology; a diagnosis.

And there are aspects of transvestic behaviour that raise discomfort and distaste, particularly the seemingly sexualised elements. Before moving on to debunk a few myths in this matter and presenting an alternative conceptualisation, I would like to reiterate the point made at the start of this book that many of the early theorists based their ideas solely on the poor troubled souls who presented at their door. These theories were not representative of all people who may have used cross-gendered clothing as a means of expressing the self.

To present an alternative conceptualisation then, to challenge the myths around fetishism; autogynephillia and the notion of cross-dressing as merely onanistic narcissism I offer the following. If, for a handful of individuals, those explanations and diagnosis sit well, then fair enough, however, there is clearly much more to be understood about the drive and the experience of cross-gendered identity than the notion of mere sexual kink for the remaining majority.   Interestingly, researchers like Richard Ekins and Victoria Prince demonstrated that in cases where transgender individuals were given more open access to a female wardrobe then the so-called fetishistic element disappeared.   Effectively there is no breaking of the taboo therefore no need to get over-excited and eroticise it.   If there is an erotic charge associated with the early experiences of cross-dressing we might easily make sense of this in terms of the psychological struggle to overcome strict taboos and internalised shame.

The effect of the neuro-transmitter dopamine (the so called 'reward neurotransmitter') is strongly linked with sex and orgasm, but also excitement, anticipation and risk-taking.   We might reflect on how the excitement of achieving the forbidden is reinforced then by the action of dopamine on the brain in the moments leading up to enactment and release, and then countered by prolactin which drives the 'petit mort' following orgasm and invites back the self disgust, guilt and shame.   It's a vicious circle similar in some ways to the mechanism involved with say, binge eating disorder.   The contemplation phase; the build up of anticipation against the wrestle of conscience; the raising of adrenaline and dopamine as the thought of enactment is increasingly entertained; the internal permission giving leading to the enactment; the denouement phase, the come-down and reproachment phase, the inevitable guilt and self loathing driven by internal thoughts that had forbidden the fulfilment of these desires.

When the forbidden is removed however, when there is no need for guilt, the mechanism is defused: what I am offering here is the idea that the fetish aspect of cross-dressing might be more credibly and reasonably explained in the context of our increased understanding of neuro-transmitter action which is predominantly a function of how we are thinking about a situation at any given time. The evidence supports this notion: that when female identified clothing is no longer forbidden it becomes quite normal and there is no arousal cycle. This is not to say that like anyone else, a transgender person can't have a kink – if kink didn't happen Ann Summers wouldn't be on the high street. But there's an important difference between the notion of using costume as part of kink-play and the non-erotic experiencing and presentation of a female-identified self through the adoption of cross-gender clothing. Not all cross-dressing therefore is fetishistic; only the fetishistic use is fetishistic, and does that need to be considered a 'pathology' when it occurs in the privacy of intimate space between consenting adults? Moi dis vivre et laissez vivre.

Given the association of 'transvestism' with alleged 'endless mirror gazing', it would be easy to assume that all people who cross-dress are narcissistic, in love with their own self-image, even 'autogynaphillic' (go on; find another pathology to throw at the poor soul). I'd suggest an alternative way of seeing this. In Oscar Wilde's 'The Picture of Dorian Gray' we see elements of the cross-dressing dilemma being played out albeit with a degree of paradoxical inversion. There is in this case an imagined beautiful self (the idealised female) who lives in the mirror. An ugly self, filled with guilt, shame and defectiveness lives outside the mirror but stands before it, admiring a picture of the self as beautiful. Two lives can be lived here as parallel, the ugly self carrying the burden of guilt and shame for the life lived by the beautiful self who resides upstairs, in the bedroom mirror. There is the classic Faustian pact – this enactment, parading in front of the mirror in women's clothes pursuing the hedonism of cross-dress and be damned; it's sinful but go enjoy it; allow yourself the freedom of debauched acts; but you'll pay for it when you get caught: these are all there. Dorian Gray is a terribly sad tale and we see the beauty of an individual corrupted by the influence of others, and led to unhealthy ways by others. And maybe this is true when the transgender male, endeavouring to be freed of the binary construct of male or female, meets the constraining discourses of transvestite or transsexual. What if we take an existentialist-humanistic slant on the idea promoted by Lord Henry, when he encourages Dorian to 'pursue beauty and fulfilment of the senses'? This idea or notion can easily transcend the supposed debauchery of what was promoted in the story and offers us a new freedom of self-actualisation. However, to achieve this is difficult if we don't have a model that fits, a way of being that is congruent.

With a new edition of the Diagnostic and Statistical Manual due for publication soon, debate rages as to the appropriateness of defining cross-gender identities as necessarily pathological. Feelings run strong from both sides of an argument – from the people who want medical validation so they can access insurance covered treatment, and others who say that gender identity disorder can only exist in an environment where gender is controlled and atypical gender presentations are disadvantaged or discriminated against. Thus the pathology is society's, not the individuals'.

The need historically to cross-dress (both male to female and female to male) has been bound up in the politics of clothing and fashion and in the hierarchy and status endowed upon certain aspects of clothing and attire. For a long time trousers were a male only attire and even now we still hear the expression 'wearing the trousers in that household' as denoting the person with the authority and the power. Strangely, within some organisations women are still expected to wear a skirt to work as if it's the only proper attire for their status.

Clothing is ultimately a marker of status, hierarchy, identity and role within society and thereby implicit in that is a person's gender because gender is ultimately enmeshed in all of the above categories. And certain clothing and fashion attributes remain the exclusive domain of women – the skirt being the most obvious.–although some have tried to introduce skirts for men it seems to push at a taboo that is still not ready to be broken down. Beckham might wear a sarong, Jean Paul Gaultier might produce a trendy man-skirt but it just hasn't made it onto the mainstream – yet.

Change can and does occur. I remember being excited by the feminism of the 1980's. I was happy to embrace the ideology. We started as a society to begin creating opportunities for women to broaden the modes and ways of being 'woman'. Yes we had the women who wore combats and shaved their heads, who wanted to dig roads and drive the big lorries – 'to prove the point', demonstrate the notion of 'equal to' by being 'same as'. And maybe that point needed to be proven in those ways, to get the message across before more moderate but equally liberating ways could be defined. Mostly, I recall that change occurred from outside the family unit – it was part of the mass media, it was part of an awareness that started to enter schools. These big social changes, shifts in the zeitgeist arise through the efforts of individuals who are prepared to face discrimination and challenge oppression in the greater good. When the few become many, change will occur.

But what of the future: how can we move to a place where society is ready to accept transgender identities, to understand this as a natural and healthy phenomenon, and where transgender individuals are free to create healthy ways of being. We might look to our history and seek comparison with previous struggles to ask how is change possible? How does change occur? In my lifetime I remember well the strikes for equal pay, the rising of the feminist movement, I remember the decriminalisation of homosexuality and the coming out of famous people like Elton John, the emergence of openly gay pop groups such as Soft Cell, and the Pet Shop Boys. I think of how commonplace homophobic language and insult continue to be, and contrast this with my memory of how prevalent racism used to be. Back in the 1970's, comics on television used to make explicitly racist jokes, and a television series 'Love thy Neighbour' was based on the premise of a black family moving in to the house next door: my how we laughed - imagine! So, noting how we gradually grew in awareness through the intervening decades of the impact of racist language, society gradually accepted the idea of disavowing the use of these terms. So if calling a pupil a n***** quite rightly has you in detention, why not 'poof' or 'lezzer'? Society still has yet to properly grasp the idea of the ways that language creates oppression.

Change is occurring but change is inevitably slow and seldom entirely linear. New legislation promises to address some of these issues – particularly in schools where bullying is increasingly recognised as having the potential to create quite long term harm to an individual's sense of self and well-being. This week however, we learn in the paper that X-factor singing hopeful, 19 year old Paije Richardson was 'mercilessly tormented by school bullies who branded him gay'. (News of the world 31/10/2010) Interestingly the paper goes on to reassure us he is straight AND has had 'at least one proper girlfriend' (ooh, thank goodness!).

I'd make the point that discrimination and oppression occurs in the insensitive use of language by a process of 'othering' that arises from the creation of a label that denotes disadvantage implicit in an identity that sits outside of the dominant group ideals. Paije, mentioned above, apparently broke the rules of boy identity by being good at styling hair and being artistic and creative. This (according to his peers) apparently defined him as 'gay' and a 'wierdo'. Unhelpfully, the newspaper article effective colludes with this mindset, writing as if this behaviour is to be expected (passive hetero-normativity), rather than suggest Paije's school is somewhat backward, and failing in its duty of care to protect its pupils from homophobic and other types of bullying.

This hetero-normative policing of acceptable gender performance and presentation also extends to the physical: lately within schools, in what in some ways feels like a loss of ground in the feminist cause, we are seeing increasing evidence of a renewed reinforcement of gendered body-ideals, with increasing pressure on girls to be lollipop thin and boys to by hyper-muscular – 'pumped up': as a result, we see more girls with eating disorders such as anorexia, and increasing numbers of boys feeling the need to abuse steroids to help them achieve an exaggerated 'male' form (the latter being the so-called Roid-heads and a phenomenon known clinically as bigorexia). All is not lost however: Durham (2009) describes how education with young people can help them be more critically aware of the influence of media images on their understanding of the world, and how to appreciate the rationale and commercial forces that drive these messages. Schools and the education system as a whole can work towards ending homophobic bullying and promote the ideals of equality, and there are pockets of good practice: here in Wales for example, three schools have been recently awarded the Rainbow mark for working to stamp out discrimination and prejudice on the basis of a person's sexuality and gender identity.

If prejudice and discrimination are to be challenged and broken down then the transgender community will need to play an active part too in raising awareness and communicating a message akin to the gay-pride movement, one that demonstrates healthy ways of being transgender, of doing transgender: that transgender is a healthy and legitimate way of life. Now, to that end it may seem unkind, but I suggest that there is a responsibility too on the part of the transgender community to create and present more aesthetically pleasing ways of doing transgender, more honest and visually appealing ways of presenting the feminine, of 'male femaling', without becoming a crude parody of a woman. Image consultant, Lucille Sorella puts it with brutal honesty when she says,

"I care deeply for TG females, but I have to admit that there is one thing that really upsets me, most of the TG females I see in public look so ridiculous they make the entire transgender community look bad" (Sorella 2010)

She cites cheap wigs, dressing like a hooker, tacky make-up, walking like a horse, and 'acting nervous and awkward' as just some of the examples of mistakes made by trans-people trying to express a feminine self but lacking the finesse and thereby leaving themselves open to ridicule. It's harsh maybe, but there is truth in what she says albeit in their defence, I suggest the problem is that transgender females have invariably missed out on the group-bitchiness of teenage girlhood that taught the majority of natal females the painful lessons about what looks good, and what looks hideous. Over recent years though, a community is developing over the Internet that is creating the bank of knowledge, information and learning tools that can help overcome this. It just takes time to learn, to experiment and to find a look that works for each individual. Key to this is learning how to choose appropriate outfits, being prepared to have them modified or tailored to fit better, choosing the most appropriate hair-cut or wig, learning to do make-up properly – more is NOT better. I personally believe that with increasing numbers of confident and attractive examples of transgender people out on the streets, and being seen at work, the phenomenon will become more acceptable. It's an easier sell when the product looks good.

In writing this book, I don't claim by any means to have finite answers, to have discovered ultimate truths, merely to have posed questions and in the presentation of ideas, hopefully provoked thought. I hope to have conveyed some of the human struggle for identity, a struggle that affects us all.

I would like to think that in the process of reading this book it opens up to all, a route of exploration and discovery that inspires every one who reads it to question how they present and perform their gendered and sexual selves, ultimately to question the rules, assumptions and internal prejudices that prevent them living honest and open lives. My wish has been to present a narrative that inspires others to create more liberating ways of being the self, to embrace the humanistic ideal of self-actualisation in whatever ways are congruent to their inner spirit. I hope to have created hope.

Happy Days

As the writing of this book draws to its final conclusion I find myself reflecting on where I am now: and these are happier times for me personally. I only seldom have a requirement to entirely 'pass as male' and most the time I can sit in a gender-queer space where my feminine self is undoubtedly read to a lesser or greater extent. Most the time I wear jeans and boots, much of the time I wear make-up and perfume, and I usually have a colourful scarf and a bit of jewellery to add to the visual aesthetic. And, make no mistake, when the opportunity arises to be out in full on grrl-mode I make the most of it and I enjoy the experience.

And, I confess to doing a bit of outreach lately – I've been queer in straight contexts and the data from these experiences tells me that there is a real potential for acceptance of transgender as an identity and as a way of being, as people become better acquainted with, and more familiar with positive examples. Familiarity will breed acceptance not contempt, particularly when the idea is better understood, and the presentation congruent.

I'd been invited to co-present a workshop at the NSPCC 2010 conference 'Promoting Respectful Relationships' and here was an ideal opportunity to take transgender out into the political domain and do outreach and education. Here, I did full-on grrl-mode and here (intriguingly) I am told, one of the delegates asked my colleague of me, "why has that woman got a beard". It seems that on this occasion the dominant physical and visual cues had suggested the default biology as natal-female – at least to some: Interesting.

And then, a week or so later I was out again, this time on a training event. A charitable counselling agency wanted an input on Ethical Dilemmas in Counselling and since it's a workshop I've delivered previously for another agency I was up for it. Now, three members of the organisation knew me from the past – we'd worked or trained together several years ago. But only one knew I was out as transgender – and she confessed to me later that she wondered if I'd come in a suit and do stealth-mode. Nah; I had to wear a suit for a funeral recently but I can't think of many contexts where I'd choose to go back to that way of being: so I went as me, myself as grrl. Pink furry boots, pleated denim mini, black tights, my lush new hair, a load of silver jewellery including my Chavvy hoops (I'm a sucker for large silver hoop earrings), and a two-tone black/purple smokey-eye effect on the make-up front. Oh, and a bit of lip-gloss: gotta be done!

And ya know what – they were brill. Now the point here is that being transgender was not the issue, was not the point. The point was that I was there to do a workshop on ethical issues and dilemmas in counselling and the fact that I am transgender was neither here nor there. So we got on with the task in hand and they engaged really well. And I felt at ease. But once again was another coming out process for me – you never finish coming out, there are always situations as here, where a couple of people who knew me before had to adjust to a new visual presentation – I was greeted with a warm but confused,

"I wouldn't have recognised you"

And then Ruth, my old buddy said I looked fab and wanted to know how I'd done my smokey-eye make-up. We compared notes briefly: I took it as a massive compliment.

Others in the group, who had never known me, had to reconcile the gender queer identity but quickly engaged in the topic and embraced me with warmth and acceptance. Later, the course delegates seemingly mostly wanted to know if I was gay: it's back to the hetero-sexual matrix I guess. It nonetheless gave them a chance to know a transgender person in the flesh so to speak, to normalise the idea. They were fine with that.

The day after the ethics course saw me walking through Cardiff city centre on a Saturday morning, again doing the full-on grrl-mode only this time I was attending and contributing to the launch of the Gender Fluidity project held by the LGBT Excellence Centre, based here in Wales. I parked up on the outskirts of town, touched up my make-up and then walked through town to the library: out and proud. I had noted on my journey in, the contrast between the early days of driving to a town where I was going to be 'out' and being very much aware of the anxiety and the un-assuredness. This occasion reminded me that increasingly there is an absence of that tension, that uncertainty. This has felt very liberating, freeing, joyous.

Walking through town was really straightforward, normal kinda. I was fine and I was enjoying being me, enjoying the feel of being this way, I was fully inhabiting my body as female and moving it in female ways. I was owning the right to be me, the right to walk through town as a trans-grrl, and I carried an expression that drifted seamlessly between nonchalance, and anarchic humour depending on the expression of the person approaching me at any given point. A light drizzle hung in the air but it dampened only my hair and not my spirits, and little more than ten minutes after leaving the car I was arriving at the launch event, buoyant and playful. The event went well and I enjoyed a few moments entertaining the audience with a short presentation, designed on the hoof and requested at short notice. It felt nice to be validated.

Later that afternoon, the event successfully launched we decamped to a local bar for a celebratory lunch and it was late afternoon before we were leaving and heading our separate ways. As I walked back through the town centre I felt at peace with the world and connected to the warmth of my inner contentment. I'd enjoyed the company of great people and been out as me, and accepted as me, and even walking back through town on my own, I retained that real sense of happiness.

I reflected on the events of that day, the myriad conversations I had enjoyed and smiled to myself at the idea of accepting an invitation to get involved in a photographic project later next year. Now, to say I have always had an aversion to having my photo taken would be something of an understatement. Over the years the photographic images have somehow never reflected back to me the self I imagined or even thought I saw in the mirror. And truth be told I was always nervous in front of the camera. I have crooked teeth so a smile is an awkward thing to do. And somehow, smiling or not, the image never quite felt right: it has to be said there are some hideous and unflattering pictures taken of me in the past – especially by supposedly professional photographers. I'd assumed cameras didn't like me, photographers even less.

So, there is a company in Cardiff that do makeovers and photo-shoots and I'd seen what they could achieve when the darling-daughter went with her girlie friends a couple of years back. I'd not given it much thought at the time but I'd been promising myself that at some point I needed to see a professional make-up artist to learn how to do stuff properly, refine the skills a bit and, since I needed a decent photo for the book cover I thought I'd give it a go.

So, I find myself in busy salon on the second floor of a building in the centre of Cardiff with a lovely girl taking me through the whole cleanse, tone, primer, foundation, make-up routine. And I can say I learned a lot in that hour. And then I meet the photographer who will do my shoot. Some people you can take one look at and feel at ease, just know they are going to be ok and I sense it in a fraction of a second with him. My first impression is right, this guy albeit armed with the camera is warm-natured, there's a genuineness about him, he's kinda sweet. He chats away, putting me at ease; we talk about me being transgender and he shares with me that he is a gay man: there's a mutual appreciation and we briefly compare notes on the coming out process. He draws a background down, asks me to stand looking up at a screen and takes a few shots, just to set the lighting levels.

Here I am, in front of a camera and for the first time I feel at ease, playful, comfortable. He clicks away busily, intersperses the shots with more friendly chat and instructions to create the shots, changes the background, alters the lights, tries another pose: it's a fluid and relaxed process: and yet in half an hour we've taken over a hundred shots. His studio is shall we say compact and bijou – a little like hiding in the under stairs cupboard but with more headroom, or being in a walk-in-wardrobe but without the hanging rails. But this is no closet, and we are both out in this space, we are both at ease in each other's company, both at ease within our selves. The shoot finally over I bid him fond farewell and go to the viewing room with an assistant to see the result of our time together. As I'm looking at these pictures I find myself really emotional – for the first time I see myself as I have somehow imagined – finally the outside self matches the inner sense of self as if the clothes have transformed the body but it's still a real body, it's a real me. The pictures tell a story of inner contentment – and that's what pictures of me have historically lacked – that inner sense of happiness.

You will no doubt have worked out by now that writing this book has been emotionally challenging and inevitably drawn up painful memories, made me revisit chapters in my life where things were less resolved, where shame and self disgust hung on my shoulders like a weighty duffle coat: yeugh, hideous times. And then I contrast this with how I am today, embracing a more congruent identity, enjoying being me and it has made me think about others less fortunate, more constrained, denied this freedom. And I knew that if I was forced to go back to passing as male full time then I'd be no different to the person who feels compelled to take the surgery route - ultimately it becomes then a choice between death or genital reassignment surgery – that these binary options would then offer the only two viable routes: choose GRS if it's what ya want, but to feel compelled seems like a sad state of affairs, a damning indictment of an inhuman society.

I have endeavoured then, both here in writing this book and in other ways, to become part of the movement that is challenging that inhumanity, creating the new ways of being: illustrating the creative possibilities – joining a new genre of social activism presenting and demonstrating transgender ways of being. I'm excited by a whole new vibe that is emerging – gender fluidity is starting to take hold as a notion, as a counter movement, as a new zeitgeist for the next generation. These creative ways of floating between genders, blending genders, queering genders is going to offer new possibilities for everyone – not just the decidedly gender confused. Now we are increasingly seeing people ready and willing to identify as transgender, to adopt positions that embody both male and female and allow the expression of a gendered self without necessarily feeling that they have to end up resorting to gender reassignment surgery, just for the right to exist. The message here is about choice and freedom to choose. This is a new language, a new identity, a new possibility. I hope this book has added positively to the voices creating and explaining this new paradigm and has gone some way towards facilitating the acceptance and awareness of transgender as an honest and creative way for people of all genders and sexualities to take courage to be themselves and tell the world. One day the world will be able to understand.

I've had some great experiences being transgender, especially lately: and the highlight for me this week was when a stunningly attractive woman in her thirties wearing very stylish and expensive clothes turns to me as a transgender grrl in her forties and says, "I love your look, I could totally wear your outfit", I think to myself, wow, mission accomplished: and these are happy days.

APPENDICES

Suggested Reading

Closets are for Clothes by Richard Harris (2010)
(www.closetsareforclothes.co.uk): A delightfully upbeat and easy
read, predominantly aimed at the lesbian/gay/bi market but
with much relevance to transgender issues –particularly for
example the sections on coming out and dealing with depression
and low self esteem.

Gender Outlaw by Kate Bornstein (1995): I love this book, not
least because it has so much honesty in it. Kate's story is
fascinating and told so openly that it offers an inspiration to
others in the transgender movement. The style of writing is very
accessible and I'd say it's a must read!

Finding The Real Me by Tracy O'Keefe and Katrina Fox (2003):
This book tells the stories of several transgender people, their
journeys, as they endeavour to find congruent ways of being. I
found this book helpful and when I looked at my bookshelves
and thought of which books I'd see as must haves for
understanding transgender then this is the second only to Gender
Outlaw above.

GenderQueer by Joan Nestle, Clare Howell and Riki Wilchins
(2002): This is a fascinating but more complex read for those

interested in the socio-polical elements of transgender. I'd
recommend it for students of gender studies and those with
academic interests in transgender.

True Selves by Mildred Brown and Chloe Ann Rounsley (2003):
This book describes itself as a guide for families, friends, co-
workers and helping professionals and although written a while
ago has some useful insights and information within.

Woman's World by Graham Rawle (2005): This is such an off-
beat, entertaining and enjoyable read and is completely accessible
to anyone. It is a novel with a transgender subtext and is just so
clever that you have to read it to believe it. I don't read novels as
a rule; however, this was the one and only exception in the past
twenty years and it earns its place on my over-crowded
bookshelves by virtue of its originality and genius.

Dress To Kill by Eddie Izzard (1998): Personal narrative and
abstract humour make this book absolutely gripping. To his
credit, Eddie is out there, making gender queer more acceptable
and visually appealing so is to be much commended on both
fronts. Top bananna.

Stepping Out Secrets by Lucille Sorella
(www.steppingoutsecrets.com): This series of booklets and
coaching videos is written to help transgender males present a
more feminine aesthetic. It covers such things as movement and
body language; hair and make-up, fashion, even voice coaching
and body shaping. Good stuff, and worth the investment.

For therapists and counsellors looking for further insight and understanding to working with queer clients I thoroughly recommend:

Davies, D (1996) 'Towards a model of Gay Affirmative Therapy' in Davies, D & Neal, C. **Pink Therapy: A Guide For Therapists Working With Lesbian, Gay and Bisexual People.** OUP. Buckingham.

Davies, D. & Neal, C. (2000) **Therapeutic Perspectives On Working With Lesbian, Gay And Bisexual Clients.** OUP Buckingham.

Davies, D. & Neal, C. (2000) **Issues In Therapy With Lesbian, Gay And Bisexual And Transgender Clients.** OUP Buckingham.

Denman, C. (2004) **Sexuality: A Biopsychosocial Approach.** Palgrave Macmillan. New York.

Martell, C., Safran, A. & Prince, S. (2004) **Cognitive Behavioural Therapies With Lesbian, Gay and Bisexual Clients.** Guildford Press. New York

Langridge, D & Barker, M. Eds.(2007) **Safe Sane & Consensual: Contemporary Perspectives on Sadomasochism.** Palgrave Macmillan, Hants.

Bader, M. (2003) **Arousal: The Secret Logic Of Sexual Fantasies** Virgin Books, London.

"If Jack the carpenter can't be king, that's sad.
If Jack the carpenter can't be Jack the
carpenter, that's tragic"

Perry, G (2004)

APPENDIX 1: OUTRAGEOUS QUOTES:

"A maid by a violent jump was changed into a man, her clitoris issuing forth. Fulgosius writes of a maid of fifteen years of age, being married, the first night her husband lay with her, was thus changed: whether it was by reason of her too much motion in the venereal act, or the fervent heat of those parts, I cannot tell; but probably it might happen by extraordinary dilation of the Clytoris, by much heat, and thereby being provok'd and by reasons of it's swelling on every side, not able to contain it self within any longer, issued out. This Clytoris lies latent within a woman's pudenda, which answers to a man's virility; this if it chance to grow over-much, may stand, instead of a man's members, yet without effusion of seed"

C17 medical advice in Peakman (2004)

"Not all homosexuals indulge in active sexual relations, a fact that should be borne in mind by those who tend to regard homosexuals as necessarily evil people who should be shunned"

Chesser, E. (1964) p183

"those who demand [sex reassignment surgery] are generally men who have given up all hope of competing with other males on anything approaching equal terms"

Storr, A. (1964) p62

Another form of treatment that might be considered is castration. - loss of testosterone would undoubtedly drastically reduce the number of orgasms the transvestite enjoys from the fetishistic aspect of his perversion

Stoller R. (1968).p246

"When Suzy [aged 17 months] began to shower with her parents, she also started to hold food in her mouth while being fed. Her cheeks puffed, she retained the food in spite of her mother's mounting irritation. We speculate that this behaviour was related to a fantasy of acquiring a penis by eating one"
                                    Roiphe, H. & Galenson, E. (1981) p137

"Whilst effeminacy may be partly genetic in cause it can be caused environmentally, by the combination of dominant mother and a hostile or remote father as the stories of Elton John and John Gielduid suggested."
                                                        James, O (2002) p99

"the reason for intervention [in the case of a boy with gender disturbance] is to prevent severe sexual problems of adulthood such as transsexualism and homosexuality" ....*"if the psychopathology of 'gender identity disorder of childhood' is one of the major etiological precursors to adulthood homosexual orientation disturbance (as the research indicates at present) it would now appear logical that homosexuality per se be re-examined as a mental disorder"*
                                                        Rekers (1995)

APPENDIX 2: THE JOHN/JOAN CASE:

David Reimer was one of twin boys born in 1965. At 6 months old he suffered a medical accident when his penis was severely mutilated in a botched circumcision. A reconstruction of the penis was not possible in those days so doctors (under the guidance of John Money) decided to construct female genitalia and instruct the parents to raise the child as a girl. Money's theory was that gender was entirely a function of how a child was raised and some argue that this opportunity gave him the perfect chance to prove this - a twin study - one raised as boy, the other as girl.

Heralded as a success, for a long time this case was cited as proof of the theories of Money and the work of the John Hopkins clinic. This was until 1997 when a TV documentary blew the lid off the whole deception. David (being raised as 'Brenda') had never been comfortable in his assigned gender and on learning the truth from his parents at 13 decided to assume masculine identity. In the following years he married and lived as a man, despite having to undergo series of operations to reverse the earlier sex reassignment. Sadly, following a combination of life events including the death of his twin he took his own life in 2004.

Ultimately, the paradox of this case is that it provided data that proved the reverse hypothesis. It has however added weight to those who assert that core gender identity is a function of brain differentiation due to prenatal and early hormones and gone some way towards introducing changes in the way inter-sex conditions are viewed and treated.

I noted with interest that there is no mention of this pivotal case in Money's book 'Gendermaps' (Money 1995).

APPENDIX 3: Non-Western 'Third Sex' Categories

"While contemporary societies still seem determined to polarize gender along strictly anatomical lines, the vast majority of cultures throughout history and around the globe understood that anatomical sex does not dictate gender identification any more than it does sexual orientation" (Bolin 1996: p22)

Table of Third Sex Categories in Non Western Cultures

Role:	Culture
Hijra	India
Khushra	Pakistan
Acault	Burma
Xanith	Oman
Mahu	Polynesia
Two-Spirit (Winkte, Berdache) Indian	North American
Female Husband	Bantu
Shamanism	Various
Eunuchs	

From: Denny, D. (1997) 'Transgender:Some Historical, Cross-Cultural, And Contemporary Models And Methods Of Coping And Treatment' in Bullough, B., Bullough, V.L. & Elias, J. **Gender Blending.** Prometheus Books. New York

REFERENCES:

Acroyd, P. (1979) **Dressing Up. Transvestism and Drag: The History Of An Obsession.** Thames and Husdon, London.

Arndt, A. (1991) **Gender Disorders And The Paraphilias.** International Universities Press, Madison.

Atkinson, R. L., Atkinson, R. C. Smith, E. E., Bem, D. J. & Nolen-Hoeksema, S. (1996) **Hilgard's Introduction To Psychology 12th Ed**. Harcourt Brace Publishers. Fort Worth.

Auyeung, B., Baron-Cohen, S., Ashwin,E., Knickmeyer, R., Taylor, K., Hacket, G., & Hines, M. (2009) **Fetal Testosterone Predicts Sexually Differentiated Childhood Behaviour In Girls and Boys**. Journal of Psychological Science Febraury 2009 20:144-148

Auyung, B., Taylor, K., Hackett, G., & Baron-Cohen, S. (2010) **Foetal Testosterone And Autistic Traits In 18 To 24 Month Old Children**. Journal of Molecular Autism 1:11

Bader, M. (2003) Arousal: **The Secret Logic Of Sexual Fantasies**. Thomas Dunne books, New York.

Bakwin, H. & Bakwin, R. M. (1953) 'Homosexual Behaviour In Children' cited in McConaghy, N. (1993) **Sexual Behaviour: Problems and Management** Plenum Press. New York

Barker, M (2007) 'Turning The World Upside-down: Developing A Tool For Training About SM' in Barker, M. & Langridge, D. **Safe, Sane And Consensual: Contemporary Perspectives On Sadomasochism.** Palgrave Macmillan. Basingstoke

Baron-Cohen, S. (2004) **The Essential Difference: Men, Women And The Extreme Male Brain.** Penguin. Middlesex.

Bem, S.L (1974) **The Measurement Of Psychological Androgyny.** Journal Of Counselling & Clinical Psychology 42, 155-162.

Blanchard, R., & Lippa, R. A. (2007). **Birth Order, Sibling Sex Ratio, Handedness, and Sexual Orientation of Male and Female Participants in a BBC Internet Research Project**. Archives of Sexual Behavior, 36, 163-176.

Bland, J. (1993) **The Gender Paradox.** Derby TV/TS Group. Belper, Derby.

Bland, J. (2004) **Transvestism And Cross-Dressing: Current Views.** Beaumont Trust. London

Bloom, A. (2002) **Conservative Men In Conservative Dresses: The World Of Cross-Dressers Is For The Most Part A World Of Traditional Men, Traditional Marriages, And Truths Turned Inside Out.** The Atlantic Monthly. Vol 289(4):94-102. on

http://www.questia.com/PM.qst?action=print&docId=50024480
32 viewed 9/12/07

Bolin, A. (1994) 'Transcending and Transgendering: Male to
Female Transsexuals, Dichotomy and Diversity' in Herdt, G.
**Third Sex, Thrid Gender: Beyond Sexual Dimorphism In
Culture And History.** Zone Books. New York

Bolin, A. (1996)'Traversing Gender: Cultural Context And
Gender Practices' in Ramet, S. P. **Gender Reversals and Gender
Cultures: Anthropological and Historical Perspectives.**
Routledge. London.

Bolin, A. (1997) 'Transforming Transvestism and Transsexualism:
Polarity, Politics and Gender' in Bullough, B., Bullough, V.L. &
Elias, J. **Gender Blending.** Prometheus Books. New York
Bolton, A. (2003) **Bravehearts: Men In Skirts.** V&A Publications.
London.

Bond, T (2004) **Ethical Guidelines for Researching Counselling
and Psychotherapy.** BACP, Rugby.

Bornstein, K (1994) **Gender Outlaw: On Men, Women And The
Rest Of Us.** Routledge. London

Bornstein, K. (1998) **My Gender Workbook.** Routeldge. London.

Brace, N. Kemp, R. & Snelgar, R. (2006) **SPSS For Psychologists.
3rd Ed.** Palgrave Macmillan. Basingstoke.

Bridget, J. & Hodgson, A (2007) **Closeted And Vulnerable: Understanding The Needs of Emerging Lesbian Gay And Bixsexual Young People.** Journal: Counselling Children & Young People. December 2007: p2-12

Brierly, H (1979) **Transvestism: A handbook With Case Studies For Psychologists, Psychiatrists, And Counsellors**. Pergamon Press, Oxford

Brizendine, L. (2007) **The Female Brain.** Bantam Press. London

Brown, G.; Wise, T.; Thomas, N.; Costa, P.; Herbst, J.; Fagan, P; & Schmidt, C. (1996) **Personality Characteristics and Sexual Functioning of 188 Cross-Dressing Men.** Journal of Nervous & Mental Disease 184(5):265-273.

Brown, M. & Rounsley, C.A. (2003) **True Selves: Understanding Transsexualism - For Families, Co-Workers And Helping Professionals.** Jossey-Bass. San Fransisco

Bullough, V.L., Bullough, B., & Smith, R. (1983) **A Comparative Study of Male Transvestites, Male to Female Transsexuals, and Male Homosexuals.** Journal of Sexual research 19:238-257

Bullough, V.L, & Bullough, B. (1993) **Cross Dressing, Sex And Gender.** University of Pennsylvania Press. Philadelphia

Bullough, B., Bullough, V.L. & Elias, J. (1997) **Gender Blending.** Prometheus Books. New York

Butler, J. (1993) **Bodies That Matter: On The Discursive Limits Of Sex.** Routledge. London.

Butler, J. (2007) **Gender Trouble. 2ⁿᵈ Ed.** Routledge. Abingdon, Oxon.

Cauldwell, D.O. (1949) **What's Wrong With Transvestism?** International Journal of Trangenderism Vol.5 issue 2 June 2001. On http://www.symposion.com/ijt/cauldwell/cauldwell_01.htm viewed 8/11/07

Chesser, E. (1964) **Sexual Behaviour.** Transworld Publishers. London

Clark-Carter, D. (2004) **Quantitative Psychological Research: A Student's Handbook.** Psychology Press. Hove.

CPCAB (2007) **Tutor User Guide: Level 4 Diploma In Therapeutic Counselling.** Counselling and Psychotherapy Central Awarding Body. Glastonbury.

Coleman, V. (1996) **Men In Dresses: A Study Of Transvestism/Crossdressing.** European Medical Journal Special Monograph. On http://vernoncoleman.com/downloads/mid.htm viewed 28/12/07

Cops Wife (2010) **My Son Is Gay!** http://nerdyapplebottom.com/2010/11/02/my-son-is-gay viewed 9/11/10

Coren, S. (1982) **Left Hander: Everything You Need To Know About Left-Handedness.** Free Press. New York.

Cozens, C. (2000) **Beginning Perl.** Wrox Press. Birmingham

Davies, D (1996) 'Towards a model of Gay Affirmative Therapy' in Davies, D & Neal, C. **Pink Therapy: A Guide For Therapists Working With Lesbian, Gay and Bisexual People.** OUP. Buckingham.

Davies, D. & Neal, C. (2000a) **Therapeutic Perspectives On Working With Lesbian, Gay And Bisexual Clients.** OUP Buckingham.

Davies, D. & Neal, C. (2000b) **Issues In Therapy With Lesbian, Gay And Bisexual And Transgender Clients.** OUP Buckingham.

Davies, D. (2007) **Not In Front Of The Students.** Therapy Today Vol 18(1) :18-21.

Denman, C. (2004) **Sexuality: A Biopsychosocial Approach.** Palgrave Macmillan. New York.

Denny, D. (1997) 'Transgender:Some Historical, Cross-Cultural, And Contemporary Models And Methods Of Coping And Treatment' in Bullough, B., Bullough, V.L. & Elias, J. **Gender Blending.** Prometheus Books. New York

Devor, A. (2004) **Witnessing And Mirroring: A Fourteen Staged Model Of Transexual Identity Formation**. Journal of Gay and Lesbian Psychotherapy, vol.8 no.1-2 ; 41-67

Doctor, R.F. & Prince, V. (1997) **Transvestism: A Survey of 1032 Cross-Dressers.** Archives of Sexual Behaviour Vol 26(6) 590-605

Doorn, C. D., Poortinga, A.M. & Verschoor, A.M. (1994) **Cross-Gender Identity In Transvestites And Male Transsexuals.** Archives of Sexual Behaviour Vol. 23 (2) 185-193.

Drescher, J (2010) **Queer Diagnosis: Parallels and Contrasts in the History of Homosexuality, Gender Variance, and the Diagnostic and Statistical Manual.** Archives of Sexual Behaviour Vol. 39 427-460.

Drummond, A. (2008) **T-Girls, Timocracy and Therapist's Taxonomies:** MSc Dissertation. Bristol University.

Durden-Smith, J. & deSimone, D. (1983) **Sex And The Brain.** Pan Books. London.

Durham, M.G. (2009) **The Lolita Effect.** Duckworth Overlook, London

Dyer, C. (1995) **Beginning Research In Psychology: A Practical Guide To Research Methods And Statistics.** Blackwell. Oxford

Dzelme, K. & Jones, R. A. (2001) **Male Cross-Dressers in Therapy: A Solution Focussed Perspective for Marriage and Family Therapists.** American Journal of Family Therapy 29:293-305

Ekins, R. (1997) **Male Femaling: A Grounded Theory Approach To Cross-Dressing And Sex-Changing.** Routledge. London

Ellis, H. (1959) **Psychology of Sex.** Pan. London

Evans, J. (2005) **How To Do Research: A Psychologists Guide.**
Psychology Press. New York

Faul, F., Erdfelder, E., Lang, A.-G., & Buchner, A. (2007).
**G*Power 3: A flexible statistical power analysis program for the
social, behavioral, and biomedical sciences.** *Behavior Research
Methods, 39,* 175-191. accessed on 4/3/08 at:
http://www.psycho.uni-
duesseldorf.de/abteilungen/aap/gpower3

Fausto-Sterling, A. (2000) **Sexing The Body: Gender Politics And
The Construction Of Gender.** Basic Books. New York.

Fee, A.(2006) **'Transgendered Identities'.** Therapy Today BACP
Lutterworth. (Vol.17, no.1 p40-42)

Field, A. & Hole, G. (2003) **How To Design And Report
Experiments** Sage. London.

Fine, C. (2010) **Delusions of Gender: The Real Science Behind
Sex Differences.** Icon. London.

Fraley, R.C (2004) **How To Conduct Behavioural Research Over
The Internet: A Beginner's Guide To HTML and CGI/Perl.**
Guilford Press. London.

Frosh, S., Phoenix, A., Pattman, R. (2002) **Young Masculinities:
Understanding Boys in Contemporary Society.** Palgrave.
Basingstoke.

Garber, M. (1997) **Vested Interests: Cross Dressing And
Cultural Anxiety.** Routledge. New York

Gosselin, C. & Wilson, G. (1980) **Sexual Variations: Fetishism, Transvestism and Sado-masochism.** Faber & Faber. London.

Haslam, M.T. (2001) **Transvestism and Cross Dressing: Towards An Understanding.** Beaumont Trust, London.

Haywood, C. & Mac an Ghaill, M (2003) **Men and Masculinities.** OUP. Buckingham.

Herdt, G. (1996) **Third Sex, Thrid Gender: Beyond Sexual Dimorphism In Culture And History.** Zone Books. New York

Heron, J. & Reason, P (1997) **A Participative Inquiry Paradigm.** Qualitative Inquiry, 3(3), 274-294.

Jurgensen, M.,Hiort, O., Holterhus, P.M. & Thyen, U (2007) **Gender Role Behaviour In children With XY Karotype And Disorders Of Sex Development.** Journal of Hormonal Behaviour 51(3) 443-53

Hinton, P. R. (2004) **Statistics Explained 2nd Ed.** Routledge. London.

Hite, S (1981) **The Hite Report on Male Sexuality.** Ballantyne. New York

Hite, S (1994) **The Hite Report on The Family.** Grove Press. New York

Holt,C.L & Ellis, J.B (1998) **Assessing The Current Validity Of The Bem Sex-Role Inventory.** Sex Roles: A Journal Of Research 39,11-12

Howells, K. (1984) **The Psychology Of Sexual Diversity.** Blackwell. Oxford

Hunt & Jensen (2007) **The Experiences Of Young Gay People In Britain's Schools** Stonewall. London.

Izzard, E. Quantick, D. & Double, S. (1998) **Eddie Izzard: Dress To Kill.** Virgin Books. London.

Izzard, E. (2003) **From Eddie to Sexie By Design.** The Times. 6/12/03 'Body and Soul. P6-7

Jacobs, M. (1998) **The Presenting Past: The Core of Psychodynamic Counselling and Therapy** OUP. Buckingham

James, O. (2002) **They Fuck You Up: How To Survive Family Life.** Bloomsbury. London.

Jones, W. & Perry, G. (2006) **Grayson Perry: Portrait Of The Artist As A Young Girl.** Chatto & Windus. London.

King, M. (2003) **Mental Health and Social Wellbieng Of Gay Men, Lesbians and Bi-sexuals in England And Wales: A Summary Of Findings.** Mind. London.

King, M., Semlyen, J., Killaspy, H., Nazareth, I. & Osborn, D. (2007) **A Systematic Review Of Research On Counselling And**

Psychotherapy for Lesbian, Gay, Bisexual And Transgender People. BACP. Lutterworth.

Kinsey, A. C., Pomeroy, W. B., Martin, C.E. & Gebhard, P. H (1953) **Sexaul Behaviour in The Human Female.** Saunders & Co. Philadelphia.

Kruijver, F.P.M, Zhou, J.N, Pool, C.W, Hofman, M.A, Gooren, C.W & Swaab, D.F (2000) **Male-To-Female Transsexuals Have Female Neuron Numbers In Limbic Nucleus.** Journal Of Clinical Endocrinology & Metabolism Vol 85(5) 2034-2041.

Kunzle, D. (2006) **Fashion and Fetishism** Sutton Publishing, Stroud.

Lance, L (2002) **Acceptance of Diversity in Human Sexuality: Will The Strategy Reducing Homophobia Also Reduce Discomfort Of Crossdressing?** College Student Journal. Vol 36 on
http://www.findarticles.com/p/articles/mi_m0FCR/is_4_36/ai_96619966/pg2
Viewed 11/11/07.

Lebow, J (2006) **Research For The Psychotherapist: From Science To Practice.** Routledge. New York

Lee, V. (2005) **He Or She: The View Is Better When You're On The Fence.** Way Out Publishing. London.

Limentani, A. (1998) **Between Freud And Klein: The Psychoanalytic Quest for Knowledge and Truth. (2nd ed.)** Karnac. London.

Lippa, R (2005) **Gender, Nature and Nurture.** Laurence Erlbaum Assoc. New York

Maguire, M. (2004) **Men, Women, Passion And Power: Gender Issues In Psychotherapy.** Brunner Routledge. Hove.

Manning, J. T. (2008) **The Finger Book: Sex, Behaviour and Disease Revealed In The Fingers.** Faber & Faber. London.

Martell, C., Safran, A. & Prince, S. (2004) **Cognitive Behavioural Therapies With Lesbian, Gay and Bisexual Clients.** Guildford Press. New York

Martino, W. & Palotta-Chiarolli, M (2003) **So What's A Boy: Addressing Issues Of Masculinity And Schooling.** OUP. Maidenhead

McConaghy, N. (1993) **Sexual Behaviour: Problems and Management** Plenum Press. New York

McLeod, J. (2003) **Doing Counselling Research 2ⁿᵈ Ed.** Sage. London

McManus, C. (2002) **Right Hand, Left Hand: The Origins of Asymmetry in Brains, Bodies, Atoms and Cultures.** Wiedenfeld & Nicolson. London.

Michel, S. (1987) 'American Women and the Democratic Family' in Higonnet, M. R., Jenson, J., Michel, S. & Weitz, M. C. **Behind The Lines: Gender and The Two World Wars.** Yale University Press. New Haven.

Mitchell, J. (2000) **Mad Men And Medusas: Reclaiming Hysteria.**
Perseus Books. New York

Moir, A. & Moir, B. (1998) **Why Men Don't Iron: The Real
Science Of Gender Studies.** Harper Collins. London

Money, J. (1995) **Gendermaps: Social Constuctionism, Feminism
and Sexosophical History.** Continuum. New York.

Moorhead, J. (2007) **Tomboys: Girls Will Be Boys.** The Times
Magazine, 4th August 2007. London.

Morrison, J. (1995) **DSM IV Made Easy: The Clinician's Guide
To Diagnosis** Guildford Press. London.

Moser, C. & Kleinplatz, P.J (2002) **Transvestic Fetishism:
Psychopathology or Iatrogenic Artifact?** New Jersey
Psychologist, 52(2) 16-17 on
http://www2.hu-berlin.de/sexology/BIB/TVFet.htm viewed
21/1/08

Mustanski, B.S.; Chivers, M.L; & Bailey, J.M. (2002) **A Critical
Review of Recent Biological Research On Human Sexual
Orientation.** Annual Review of Sex Research 13:89-140.

Nestle, J. Howell, C. & Wilchins, R. (2002) **GenderQueer: Voices
From Beyond The Gender Binary.** Alyson Books. New York.

O'Keefe, T. (1999) **Sex, Gender And Sexuality: 21st Century
Transformations.** EPP. London

O'Keefe, T & Fox, K. (2003) **Finding The Real Me: True Tales Of Sex And Gender Diversity.** Jossey-Bass. San Fransisco

Pallant, J. (2001) **SPSS Survival Guide: A Step By Step Guide To Data Analysis Using SPSS For Windows (Version 10).** Open University Press. Maidenhead.

Peakman, J. (2004) **Lascivious Bodies: A Sexual History of the Eighteenth Century.** Atlantic Books. London

Perlman, G. (2003) 'Gay Affirmative Practice' in C. Lago and B. Smith (eds) **Anti-Discriminatory Counselling Practice,** London:Sage, pp50-61.

Perry, G (2004) **Turner Prize Winner Charts His Insecurities In Pottery.** The Independent 15/10/04 p16-17

Phillips, H. (2001) **Boy Meets Girl.** New Scientist. No.2290, p29-35

Pinker, S. (2008) **The Sexual Paradox: Troubled Boys, Gifted Girls And The Real Difference Between The Sexes.** Atlantic Books. London.

Ramet, S. P. (1996) **Gender Reversals and Gender Cultures: Anthropological and Historical Perspectives.** Routledge. London.

Rammsayer, T. H. & Troche, S.J (2006) **Sexual Dimorphism In The Second To Fourth Digit Ratio And Its Relation To Gender-Role Orientation In Males And Females. Journal Of Personality And Individual Differences** Vol.42:6. p911-920

Reason, P (1998) **A Participatory Worldview**. Resurgence, 168
42-44, on
http://people.bath.ac.uk/mnspwr/Papers/Paricipatoryworld.ht
m accessed 6/7/08

Reed, T. (2006) **Atypical Gender Development: A Review.**
International Journal Of Transgenderism, 9(1) p29-44

Reisbig, A.M.J. (2007) **The Lived Experiences Of Adult Children
Of Cross-Dressing Fathers: A Retrospective Account.** Doctoral
theses: Kansas State University.
On http://www.krex.k-
state.edu/dspace/bitstream/2097/303/1/AllisonReisbig2007.pd
f viewed 28/12/07.

Rekers, G.A (1985) **Gender Identity Disorder** from
http://www.leaderu.com/jhs/rekers.html viewed Nov 07

Renold, E. (2005) **Girls, Boys and Junior Sexualities: Exploring
Children's Gender And Sexual Relations In The Primary
School.** RoutledgeFalmer. London.

Roiphe, H. & Galenson, E. (1981) **Infantile Origins Of Sexual
Identity.** International Universities Press. New York.

Salkind, N.J. (2008) **Statistics For People Who Think They Hate
Statisitics 3rd Ed.** Sage. London

Schaub, M. & Williams, C. (2007) **Examining the Relations
Between Masculine Gender Role Conflict and Men's**

Expectations About Counselling. Psychology of Men & Masculinity. Vol 8 1, 40-52.

Schaivi, M. R. (2004) **A Girlboy's Own Story: Non-Masculine Narrativity In 'Ma Vie En Rose'.** College Literature 31,3:1-26 on http://www.findarticles.com/p/search?tb=art&qt=%22Schiavi%2C+Michael+R%22 viewed May2007.

Schott, R. (1995) **The Childhood and Family Dynamics of Transvestites.** Archives of Sexual Behaviour 24:3, 309-321

Shaw, L. Butler, C. & Marriot, C. (2008) **Sex And Sexuality Teaching In Clinical Psychology Courses.** Clinical Psychology Forum (187, July 2008):7-11

Showalter, E. (1987) 'Rivers and Sassoon: The Inscription of Male Gender Anxieties' in Higonnet, M. R., Jenson, J., Michel, S. & Weitz, M. C. **Behind The Lines: Gender and The Two World Wars.** Yale University Press. New Haven.

Skinner, R. & Cleese, J (1983) **Families And How To Survive Them.** OUP. New York

Sorella, L. (2010) **Stepping Out Secrets** http://www.steppingoutsecrets.com viewed Nov 2010.

Spargo, T (1999) **Foucault and Queer Theory.** Icon Books. Cambridge.

Steinskog, E. (2008) **Voice of Hope: Queer Pop Subjectivities** on **http://trikster.net/1/steinskog/1.html** viewed Aug 2009

Stoller, R.J. (1968) **Sex And Gender: On The Development Of Masculinity And Femininity.** Science House. New York.

Stoller, R.J.(1996) 'The Gender Disorders' in Rosen, I. **Sexual Deviation 3rd Ed.** OUP. Oxford.

Stone, A. (1998) **Seeing : A Film With No Romance, No Aliens, And No Famous Stars Provides A New Understanding Of Human Sexuality.** Boston Review. January **1998 on** http://www.bostonreview.net/BR22.6/Stone.html viewed 28/12/07

Storr, A. (1964) **Sexual Deviation.** Penguin. Middlesex

Stryker, S. & Whittle, S Ed. (2006) **The Transgender Studies Reader.** Routledge. New York.

Suthrell, C. (2004) **Unzipping Gender: Sex, Cross-Dressing And Culture.** Berg, Oxford

Walker, M (2000)'Foreword' in Davies, D. & Neal, C. (2000b) **Issues In Therapy With Lesbian, Gay And Bisexual And Transgender Clients.** OUP Buckingham.

Whittle, S. (2000) **The Transgender Debate: The Crisis Surrounding Gender Identities.** Garnet Publishing. Reading

Wilchins, R. (2004) **Queer Theory, Gender Theory: An Instant Primer.** Alyson Publications. California.

Wilson, C.J, Chung,. I, De Vries, & G.J, Swaab, D.F. (2002) **Sexual Differentiation Of The Bed Nucleus Of The Stria Terminalis In**

Humans May Extend Into Adulthood. Journal Of Neuroscience 22(3):1027-1033

Wilson, G & Rahman, Q. (2005) **Born Gay: The Psychobiology of Sex Orientation.** Peter Owen. London.

Wise, T. T. & Meyer, J.K. (1980) **The Border Area Between Transvestism and Gender Dysphoria: Transvestic Applicants for Sex Reassighment.** Archives of Sexual Behaviour Vol 9.(4): 327-342

Woodhouse, A (1989) **Fantastic Women: Sex, Gender And Transvestism.** Macmillan. Basingstoke.

Zandvliet, T. (2000) 'Transgender Issues in Therapy' in Davies, D. & Neal, C. (2000) **Issues In Therapy With Lesbian, Gay And Bisexual And Transgender Clients.** OUP Buckingham.

Zucker, K.J. & Blanchard. R. (1997)'Transvestite Fetishism: Psychopathology and Theory' in Laws, D.R & O'Donohue, W. **Sexual Deviance: Theory, Assessment and Treatment.** Guildford Press. New York.

Lightning Source UK Ltd.
Milton Keynes UK

176599UK00003B/81/P